Pub Walks in the Cotswolds

Laurence Main

Published by Sigma Leisure – an imprint of
Sigma Press, 1 South Oak Lane, Wilmslow, Cheshire SK9 6AR, England.

Whilst every effort has been made to ensure that the information given in this book is correct, neither the publisher nor the author accept any responsibility for any inaccuracy.

British Library Cataloguing in Publication Data
A CIP record for this book is available from the British Library.

ISBN: 1-85058-303-X

Typesetting and Design by: Sigma Press, Wilmslow, Cheshire.

For the technically minded: the author's typewritten text was scanned electronically prior to input to a DTP system; initial spell-checking and grammatical analysis were performed with the aid of 'Grammatik V' software, with human assistance as appropriate!

Maps by: Morag Perrott

Text photographs: Chris Rushton

Cover photograph: The Old Crown Inn, Uley, Dursley – see walk 18.

Printed by: The Cromwell Press, Melksham, Wiltshire

CONTENTS

The Cotswolds

The designation 'Area of Outstanding Beauty' is not unique in Britain. Many walkers find the Cotswolds area the most satisfying to walk in, however. It forms the widest part of the belt of Oolitic limestone which connects the English Channel with the North Sea. The old county of Gloucestershire contained most of the Cotswolds. This is now divided into Gloucestershire and Avon, while Worcestershire, Oxfordshire and Wiltshire also have bits.

Geology and Geography

The tilted plateau averages about 600 ft above sea level, which can make it a cold, windy place. The western escarpment is dissected in places by river valleys, as at Stroud, where the steep gradients cause the fast-flowing streams that attracted the woollen mills. Most of the Cotswolds are drained by the River Thames and its tributaries, such as the Churn, the Coln, the Windrush and the Evenlode, in the east. Where the streams flow westwards they have cut into the scarp slope so that outlying areas such as Cam Long Down and Bredon Hill are now detached.

The Cotswolds spring from the Jurassic era (100-170 million years ago), when this area had a subtropical climate and was covered by the sea. The limestone is comprised of Inferior Oolite which is older than and below the Great Oolite. 'Egg stones', rounded spheres of calcium carbonate, make up the Inferior Oolite, which makes a good building stone. Even better is the Great Oolite, which is hard and white and you can see it at such places as Blenheim Palace and Windsor Castle. Stonesfield Slate, which was used for the traditional Cotswold tiles, and Fuller's Earth (so necessary for cleansing wool and felting cloth) form layers between these two limestones.

People and History

Stone, used to build houses and walls, is the characteristic feature of the Cotswolds. Its use dates back to at least 2500 BC with the dry-stone walling in Belas Knapp Long Barrow. Most modern houses in the Cotswolds conform to the traditional architecture but they are usually built of reconstituted stone and roofed with moulded tiles. A few quarries are still working – but not enough to give serious cause for concern to the environment.

The Cotswolds were wooded until farmers settled here about 5000 years ago. These New Stone Age people constructed dozens of long barrows. Conventional archaeology has failed to solve the riddle of why a small population of subsistence farmers should devote so much of their time and energy to creating these huge cairns of stones, complete with internal dry-stone walls. The answer is more likely to be found by dowsers and ley-hunters. They try to come to these sacred spots with the eyes and feelings of our ancestors who felt respect for the earth as a living being. Hundreds of smaller round barrows can be found, often with trees now growing on them. These date from the Bronze Age but appear on leys (alignments of ancient sites) along with pre-Reformation churches that stand on pre-Christian holy places. A good example of a ley can be studied on the Saintbury walk (the first walk in this book).

Hillforts abound on the western escarpment and belong to the Iron Age, from about 600 BC. They did not withstand the Romans. The local Dubunni tribe accepted Roman rule and moved from their hillforts into Roman settlements. In the case of Bourton-on-the-Water they hardly moved at all. Cirencester grew to become one of the greatest Roman cities in northwestern Europe. Roads radiated from it, such as the Fosse Way, Ermin Way and Akeman Street. The Romans take the credit for such routes. Characteristically straight sections have been incorporated into the modern road network, although the British had their own straight highways 500 years before, in the days of Molmutius. Scattered around Cirencester were villas such as at Chedworth. Their prosperity continued well into the fifth century, but the population was reverting to Iron Age lifestyles when the Saxons eventually gained their crucial victory at Dyrham in 577.

Time passes slowly in the Cotswolds and the Middle Ages are as if but yesterday. Walk through a small Cotswold town and the buildings transport you back 500 years, to the great days of the wool trade. Wooden houses were common until about 1400 and often the stone is a facade applied to a timber-framed house. Similarly, the familiar dry-stone walls date back to the enclosures of the 18th century.

The prosperity of the Cotswolds, particularly on the wide expanse of rolling hills at the Chipping Campden end, was based on the primary raw material. Descendents of the Roman long-wool sheep did well on the limestone and grew long, heavy fleeces. Their wool was reckoned to be the best in Europe and the Flemish cloth industry could not import enough of the sheepskins. Having exploited the sheep, the rich wool merchants salved their consciences by building great 'wool churches' at Cirencester, Wotton-under-Edge and Chipping Campden, and other places.

Cotswold wool underpinned the economy to such an extent that the Chancellor of the Exchequer sat on the woolsack. Abbeys at Winchcombe, Hailes, Gloucester, Tewkesbury and Bruern took up much of the land with their sheepwalks. Their great wealth was grabbed by noble families and merchants who supported Henry VIII's dissolution of the abbeys in 1539. They, in turn, spent the profits on building great houses, such as Snowshill Manor and Stanway House.

The government increasingly taxed the export of wool, both to raise revenue and to discourage the raw material going to foreign cloth makers who would sell it back to this country. The native cloth industry became more important and this shifted the centre of production to the Stroud area, where the deep valleys had swiftly-flowing streams to turn waterwheels. The Stroudwater Canal and the Thames and Severn Canal were designed to serve this industry, but the coming of steam and the Industrial Revolution saw the Cotswolds lose out to the industrial north. Therefore, the area's survival today as an unspoilt, unpolluted, area.

Cotswolds Flora and Fauna

The Cotswolds are known for their variety. Climate, geology, soil, topography and land-use all affect wildlife and its habitats. Most of the land is now given over to growing arable crops such as wheat, barley, oats, oil-seed rape and vegetables. There is also a lot of seeded pasture, while it would be interesting to know how much land is taken up by horses! Wildlife finds homes in the hedgerows and grass verges. Woodland provides cover for many creatures. Forests do exist on the dip slope, notably at Chedworth and near Colesbourne, and at Cirencester Park. It is the western escarpment that is most heavily wooded, however, because of the difficulty of ploughing its steep slopes. This means that the Cotswold Way, following the edge of the tilted plateau, is particularly rich in trees and varied landscapes.

Yellowhammer and stonechat find food and nesting sites on thickets of thorn and elderberry set in the sheepwalks. Even the grasslands can support wildlife as they remain in places unaffected by ploughing, herbicides or artificial fertilisers. Some valleys are dry, which is evidence of a wetter climate long ago, or of cutting by powerful streams of meltwater when the ground was still frozen at the end of the Ice Age. If a stream is called a winterbourne, it only has water when the water-table is high, in the winter. Undrained patches of marshy ground support sedges, rushes, marsh orchids and frogs and toads.

Beech is the commonest tree on the steep hillsides, where the ancient forest has survived. In spring it is scented by wild garlic, while in autumn the woodland paths are carpeted with leaves. Ash and oak are also common, while yew, cherry, whitebeam, hazel, holly and sycamore can all be seen. May is a good month to see the bluebells, while primroses line the tracks. Badgers exist, if unseen, and wild fallow deer roam in places. Grey squirrels are everywhere, as are foxes, voles and small mice. Woodpeckers may tap above your heads, while in spring the accompanying chorus is provided by chiffchaffs, blackcaps and garden wood warblers. Flocks of brambling fly over from Scandinavia to spend the winter eating the fallen beech seeds, known as masts. Don't be surprised to disturb a buzzard or a sparrowhawk as you turn a corner on a remote path.

Common lands near Cheltenham and Stroud, such as Cleeve Common and Minchinhampton Common, are ancient grasslands which have escaped the plough. Such 'unimproved' locations can contain over 150 different species or herbs and grasses. Purple thyme, yellow cowslips, blue harebells and white ox-eye daisies can all add a splash of colour to your walk. Butterflies are attracted to these flowers. Look out for the chalkhill and small blue butterflies, also the marbled white and grayling, the common blue, green hairstreak, meadow brown and skippers. The colourful peacock, painted lady and clouded yellow butterflies also visit these parts.

The streams and rivers of the Cotswolds contribute greatly to their character. Sparkling, clear, water over a stony bed is part and parcel of the chocolate box scenes at Bourton-on-the-Water or the Upper and Lower Slaughters. Damselflies and dragonflies abound, but the otter has now become extinct. If you do think you see one, it may be a mink. To the south and east of Cirencester are the reclaimed gravel pits which now form the Cotswold Water Park. These have become well-known for their wildlife and you may even be lucky enough to see a kingfisher.

Villages and Traditions

The villages of the Cotswolds achieve the feat of blending with the landscape. Almost all of them were established before the Norman Conquest. They were the homes of the Saxon farmers, whose domestic buildings were usually made of timber and thatch. Stone was used to build churches and some evidence of Saxon stonework has survived in a few churches. The Normans set about building manors and farms, and rebuilding churches, with the local stone. This varies in colour according to the amount of iron in the limestone strata.

The Chipping Campden and Broadway area has a honey-coloured stone but Stanways's stone is richer in iron and has a gold effect. The central wolds tend to pearly-white, while the stones of the south have a grey tint. Each village had its local quarry with its own mason, which encouraged a local identity to appear. The place-names are usually English and can be deciphered. Wotton-under-Edge nestles below the western escarpment. Cot, cott or cote refers to a cottage, while ton or tun is the Saxon for farmstead. Stan, as in Stanway and Stanton, is a reference to stone. Ship, as in Shipton, doesn't hint at some nautical connection – it means sheep.

Some villages have a centre, marked by the church, the manor and a farm, around which the houses are grouped. Others straggle along a trade route. The village green is a common feature, so that the villagers could herd their livestock together for protection. This is usually the place to find the old stocks, as at Moreton-in-Marsh. Medieval prosperity earned charters for some places to hold markets and fairs. Some thirty villages were granted borough status during the heyday of the wool trade.

Traditions have survived here, as with the annual Clipping Ceremony at Painswick and the Whitsun games at Dover's Hill. May Morning sees the Morris Men dancing in the summer at a variety of locations where the characteristic Cotswold dialect is still strong. Many newcomers have been attracted by this corner of paradise, with its slower pace to life and lack of city pressure. The effect of wealthy commuters or second-homers can, unfortunately, be seen in the loss of community facilities such as post offices and bus services that the ordinary locals need.

Great efforts are being made to continue the traditional craftwork in the Cotswolds. This is largely a result of the foresight of William Morris. Born in London in 1834, he joined the Pre-Raphaelite Brotherhood and influenced the Arts and Crafts Movement, as with Charles Ashbee's work at Chipping Campden and Gimson's and the Barnsley's at Pinbury and Daneway. Morris liked staying at Broadway Tower, from where he wrote to protest against a scheme to restore Tewkesbury Abbey. This letter inspired the foundation of the Society for the Protection of Ancient Buildings. His ideas influenced the restoration of churches as at Stanton and North Cerney. Broadway, in particular, was put on many people's maps because of Morris's enthusiasm for it.

The Cotswold Way – and other paths

Many of the walks in this book follow short sections of the Cotswold Way. They should inspire you to complete the whole Way, preferably on successive days over at least a week. This makes for a special experience which would endear anyone to both walking and the Cotswolds. Approximately 100 miles long, a route along the spectacular western escarpment of the Cotswolds was put forward as a long distance path, like the Pennine Way, in 1953 by the Gloucestershire Committee of the Ramblers' Association. This was shortly after the historic National Parks and Access to the Countryside Act of 1949, which provided for the registration of public footpaths and bridleways and for the creation of long distance paths. Now known as national trails, these attract 100% grants for the creation of new rights of way, path improvements and publicity. Tony Drake's proposed Cotswold Way was not one of the chosen routes, however.

Undaunted, Gloucestershire County Council designated the Cotswold Way itself, relying on existing rights of way. Launched during National Footpath Week in 1970, the Way was given priority for waymarking and signposting, culminating in 'Operation Cotswaymark' in 1975. All the landowners along its 100 miles had to be traced, contacted and persuaded to agree to waymark arrows being placed on their land. Miraculously, this was achieved. The official Countryside Commission waymark arrows are employed, being yellow for footpaths and blue for bridleways. A distinguishing white dot was added to these to show the route of the Cotswold Way, which was also waymarked through towns and villages with white arrows. If you come across red arrows, you are on a by-way open to all traffic. Noteworthy features include the use of a sighting board to allow walkers to follow the exact route of the right of way across a field which is on the brow of a hill.

The Cotswolds do not provide difficult walking, but they are enough to test the average walker. There is 10,000 feet of climbing involved when you walk all the way between Chipping Campden and Bath, although you only go above 1000 feet a couple of times. Good walking boots are needed, as are spare layers of clothing to cope with the wind. Waterproof clothing should always be carried, while it's reassuring to have some emergency supplies of food and drink in your rucksack. The art of backpacking is to carry the minimum, which is easier if you stay in bed and breakfast accommodation (like pubs) along the way. Many carry a tent and sleeping-bag for camping.

The best guidebook is the one by Mark Richards, published by Thornhill Press. Mark has also had a guide to the Cotswold Way published by Penguin, but it is his Thornhill Press book with its Wainwright-style strip-map that is the simplest and the best. He sought and received advice from the late great AW and his own strip-map guide is a classic in the mould of 'the Master'. Don't start at the Way's northern end in Chipping Campden and walk south to Bath, however. This will give you 100 miles of inconvenience trying to read both the strip-maps and the Ordnance Survey Maps upside down. Go to the end of the book, start at Bath and walk up each page and map northwards. This brings the bonus of the prevailing south-westerly weather at one's back and the unfolding of the Cotswold Edge as it rises to the north.

Another invaluable publication is the Cotswold Way Handbook by the Gloucestershire Area of the Ramblers' Association. This gives details of transport and accommodation and is available from R.A. Long, 27 Lambert Avenue, Shurdington, Cheltenham, Gloucestershire. Both this and Mark Richards' guide to the Cotswold Way are also available from the national office of the Ramblers' Association, 1-5 Wandsworth Road, London, SW8 2XX

Real Ale

The two smallest breweries in England are in the Cotswolds. Arkell's established Donnington Brewery in a picturesque old mill alongside a lake two miles northwest of Stow-on-the-Wold in 1865. Now an independent brewery, its beer matches the beauty of the buildings. Cirencester has a small brewery founded as recently as 1983 in some old cellars. This changed hands in 1986 and now relies on the town's Roman image. Want a dark and malty real ale? Send for a Centurion. Another independent brewery is at Uley, where the Victorian village brewery was reopened in 1985.

The gentler hill slopes of the Cotswolds used to support vines and white wine is being produced again at Charlton Court, near Tetbury. Cider was always the farm labourers' favourite drink. When the attractions of simple country living brought Ernest Gimson and his fellow-architects Sidney and Ernest Barnsley to the Sapperton area at the end of the 19th century, they did more than produce excellent furniture. While at Daneway House they made 2000 gallons of cider from one year's apple crop. Cider is still made at Smith's Fruit Farm, Chipping Campden, bringing a few intoxicating weeks of air spiced by the aroma of crushed and fermented apples in the autumn.

All of the pubs featured in this book serve real ale on draught. This means that the beers come from the brewery while they are still in the process of fermentation. Fermenting continues even while the barrels are in the pub cellar. The resulting carbon dioxide escapes through a spile hole. The beer drawn for you might come direct from the barrel as a gravity-drawn beer, or with the aid of an electric pump or hand pump attached to the bar. The only extraneous pressure applied to the beers come from these pumping actions. The heavily advertised and widely available keg beers and lagers, by contrast, have their fermentation killed off by being pasteurised and delivered in airtight, sealed kegs to the pubs. Nitrogen oxide, or carbon dioxide is then used to force the beer out of the kegs under pressure. Gassy beers and lagers are the result of much of this gas dissolving into the liquid, which is shunned by lovers of traditional real ales.

The landlord and/or cellarman have a more demanding job when looking after real ale. Fine tolerances of temperature and cleanliness have to be worked to, while the shelf-life of draught beer is very short. Training and experience are needed to acquire the skill to keep a good pint. The publican can add that magic ingredient that turns a moderate beer into a good one.

Opening Hours

Under recent legislation pubs in England can now open for a maximum of twelve hours each day on Mondays to Saturdays (being 11 a.m. to 11 p.m.) and for six and a half hours on Sundays (12 noon to 3 p.m. and 7 p.m. to 10.30 p.m.) unless extensions have been granted by local licensing magistrates. Additionally, a growing number of pubs stay open during Sunday afternoons to serve meals, with which alcohol may then be consumed on the premises.

Most country pubs do not find it in their interest to take full advantage of these 'relaxed' hours and tend to stick to the 'traditional' hours of 12 noon to 3 p.m. and 6 p.m. to 11 p.m. or 7 p.m. to 11 p.m. Wherever possible I've shown the opening hours of the pubs in this book verbatim from the mouth of the licensee; these may vary from winter to summer so, if in doubt, give the pub a ring. All the pubs are open for the maximum permitted hours on Sundays.

The Walks

Each walk in this book follows rights of way to which you, as a member of the public, have unrestricted access. These are public footpaths, bridleways and by-ways as well as lanes and roads. When surveyed, all these routes were free from any obstructions. Such a statement could be made about nearly all the paths on the map in Gloucestershire. Most of them would appear to be signposted and waymarked too. Tony Drake, the Ramblers' Association footpaths secretary in Gloucestershire, has set the rest of the country an excellent example. Hundreds of volunteers also do their bit for the Cotswolds Voluntary Warden Service. In the unlikely event of any path problems, do send full details to the Ramblers' Association (the head office is at 1 – 5 Wandsworth Road, London, SW8 2XX). They will make sure it reaches the appropriate person – Tony Drake for the Gloucestershire part of the Cotswolds, or the Cotswold Warden Office, County Planning Department, Shire Hall, Gloucester, G11 2TN, tel. 0452 425674.

In most of the Cotswolds, dogs can accompany you on walks, but some areas have signs requesting you to leave them behind or keep them on a lead, especially at lambing time. Please remember that dogs endangering livestock may be shot and the owner fined. Thoughtless walkers bringing dogs onto sheep pastures can also destroy relations between farmers and ramblers which have been patiently built up over the years and yielded cooperation over waymarking. Keep to the path, honour the Country Code, and always regard it as a privilege to walk across someone else's land; in that way, we can build an atmosphere of cooperation, not confrontation, in the countryside.

LOCATION MAP

HEREFORD & WORCESTER

N

GLOUCESTERSHIRE

CHELTENHAM

Seven
Springs
9 ●

GLOUCESTER

Painswick Hill ●10
& Stream

●14 Around
Slad

STROUD   Sapperton
                  16
Oakridge & ●   ●
Siccaridge 15
Wood

SEVERN ESTUARY

Hetty Pegler's ●18   ●19 Nailsworth
Tump   & Avening

22
Wotton-under- ●
Edge   TETBURY
                    23
AVON   ● South of
                        Tetbury

Hawkesbury ●24
Upton   25-27 see inset

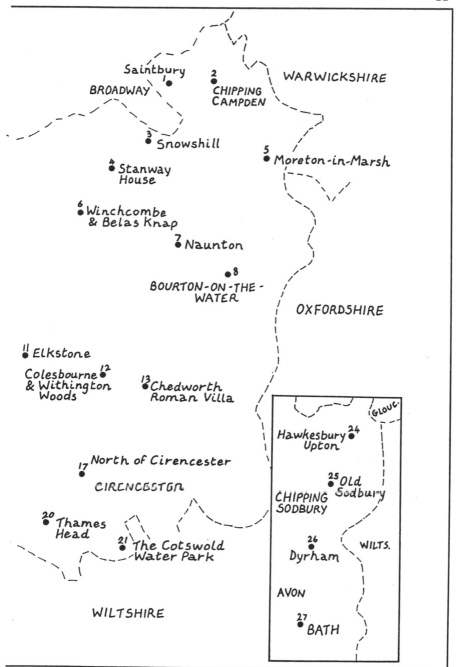

County Councils, as highway authorities, hold and maintain the definitive maps and statements that are legal proofs of public rights of way. Further information on rights of way is available from the Ramblers' Association (address above).

The walks are numbered in sequence from north to south and are spread over all of the Cotswolds. Make use of the Ordnance Survey Pathfinder maps, details of which are given for each walk. These are beautiful keys to the countryside which all walkers should become familiar with. Studying them will show where certain walks can be linked together should a longer route be desired or access to a bus stop be necessary.

❖ Walks 7 (Naunton) and 8 (Bourton-on-the-Water) meet at St. Peter's Church, Upper Slaughter to give a 15 mile walk.

❖ Walks 10 (Painswick Hill and Stream) and 14 (Around Slad) connect at St. Mary's Church, Painswick to form an 11 mile walk.

❖ Walks 12 (Colesbourne and Withington Woods) and 13 (Chedworth Roman Villa) join at Chedworth to give a walk of about 16 miles from the bus stop at Colesbourne.

❖ Walks 15 (Oakridge and Siccaridge Wood) and 16 (Sapperton) can be combined at the Daneway Inn to make a 10.5 mile walk.

All should be within the capabilities of anyone of average fitness. An average time is about two miles per hour, which allows time for short stops along the way. Do remember that the physical landscape is changing all the time, for example as hedges are grubbed up and fields amalgamated.

The Country Code
Guard against all risk of fire
Fasten all gates
Keep dogs under proper control
Avoid damaging fences, hedges and walls
Keep to paths across farmland
Leave no litter
Safeguard water supplies
Protect wildlife, wild plants and trees
Go carefully on country roads
Respect the life of the countryside

1. SAINTBURY

Route: Broadway – Bibsworth Covert – Saintbury Cross – Saintbury Church – Tumulus – Golf Course – Broadway

Distance: $5^1/_2$ miles

Maps: O.S. Pathfinders 1020 Vale of Evesham and 1043 Broadway & Chipping Campden

Start: The Crown & Trumpet Inn, Broadway (Grid Reference: SP095374)

Access: Broadway is on the A44 between Evesham and Moreton-in-Marsh.

The Crown & Trumpet Inn is in Church Street, just off the High Street, where the Horse and Hound Inn is located. Both pubs have space for car-parking and there are bus stops between them. There are several services run by Castleways, the 1989 National Award Winner of 'Best Bus Company in Britain' (tel. 0242 602949/603715). There is a good service to and from Cheltenham as well as a link with Evesham, where there is a British Rail station.

The Crown & Trumpet Inn (0386 853202)

This 17th century coaching inn serves Flowers real ales as well as fine food. Bed and breakfast is available. The opening hours are 11 a.m. to 3 p.m. and 5.30 p.m. to 11 p.m. on weekdays, 12 noon to 3 p.m. and 7 p.m. to 10.30 p.m. on Sundays.

The Horse and Hound Inn (0386 852287)

Flowers original real ale is served here, too, along with good quality food. The fireplaces and timbered beams testify to its origins as 17th century cottages. Opening hours are 11 a.m. to 11 p.m. on weekdays; 12 noon to 3 p.m. and 7pm to 10.30 p.m. on Sundays.

The Horse and Hound

Saintbury

Saintbury's name may be derived from a general feeling of holiness about the place, than from a specific saint. More mundane commentators see it as a corruption of *Swainsburgh*, meaning the fort or town of villagers, but there is good reason to favour its association with holiness.

Leys

A good example of a ley runs roughly north-south through the village. Alfred Watkins employed the term 'ley' to denote the mysterious alignments of ancient sites that he perceived as running across the country. He wrote about this in 'The Old Straight Track' (1925). His work has been taken up by others and there is now a thriving magazine entitled 'The Ley Hunter' (P.O. Box 92, Penzance, Cornwall, TR18 2XL). Its editor Paul Devereux, has written a number of books bringing the ley hypothesis up to date, including 'The Ley Guide' (Empress, 1987). This details about 3.5 miles of a ley running through Saintbury. This section was assessed statistically and found to be a deliberate alignment of a cross, a church, a tumulus and a long barrow. Bob Forrest, the statistician, wrote, 'A few more cases like this, and I shall be joining the ranks of those who ask why these lines were laid out, rather than whether or not these lines exist'.

The route takes you to the cross which is at the crossroads, north of the village. This is more than a junction between the modern B4632 and the minor road through Saintbury that continues northwards as a rough track. It is also the meeting-point of the Vale of Evesham with the Cotswolds – a good place to start this book! The cross has a 15th century shaft surmounted by a Maltese cross and sundial which date from the 19th century. It was where funeral processions stopped for a rest on their way to Saintbury Church.

Saintbury Cross

Saintbury Church is dedicated to St Nicholas and has a prominent spire, which sits on a tower in the south transept. There has been a church here since before the Norman Conquest and an octagonal stone is kept in the south transept and is reputedly an ancient, perhaps pre-Christian, altar.

It was later used as a dole table. Another old altar stone, perhaps from the Middle Ages, is kept under a Jacobean table in the north transept. The ley passes through the modern altar at the east end of the church.

Climb Willersey Hill at the back of the church to admire the view from this northern edge of the Cotswolds over the Vale of Evesham. Then, follow the path which passes within yards of a tumulus or ancient round barrow. This has suffered from ploughing since its erection in the Bronze Age, while it was excavated in 1935. The ley crosses it to run south to a Neolithic long barrow on the golf course, which is surmounted by an Iron Age hillfort. Excavated in 1884, human and ox bones were found here. Well off the route of this walk, the ley continues south over an old pagan cemetery at SP 11853680 (not marked on the O.S. Pathfinder map). It then goes on to Seven Wells Farm (SP 11943464), which is on Walk 3 in this book (see that walk's notes). It is possible that this ley extends further south.

The return leg of this walk, past the golf course, brings you to a gate overlooking an estate road. A holy well is nearby, in the direction of Farncombe. In a charter of 972, when the Saxon King Edgar gave this land to the monks of Pershore Abbey, a hermit known as Cada had a 'minster' or cell on the side of Willersey Hill. Perhaps he was drawn to a spot on the ley.

The Walk

A brief foray into Worcestershire is necessary to make the start of this walk. This is because Broadway is the best place for local bus services, connecting with British Rail at Evesham and Cheltenham, as well as being a good place for pubs. With your back to the Crown and Trumpet, go right down Church Street and turn right along Broadway's High Street. Pass the Horse and Hound on your left and continue past the B4632 road to Willersay on your left. Notice the Cotswold Teddy Bear Museum on your left, then pass a signposted public footpath on your left, just after Fenwick and Fisher Antiques. Continue past the signposted Cotswold Way on your right and, after a further 75 yards, reach another signposted public footpath on your left.

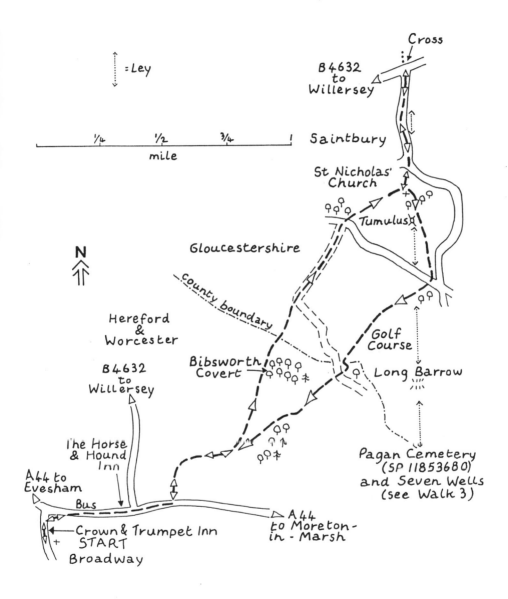

Turn left along the path which runs between two walls and passes Feel Cottage on your left. Go ahead at the next signpost to follow the path past Jasmine Cottage on your right. Cross a road and take the narrow, signposted, path ahead. Bear right with a fence on your left and a hedge on your right. Cross a footbridge ahead and continue to a small wooden gate (painted white). Go through this and veer left across a field to a gap in the hedge.

Pass through the gap in the hedge to bear left up the middle of a long field. Cross a stile in the hedge at its far end and continue beside a hedge on your right. Pass an orchard on your left. Go ahead over a stile in the corner and cross a small stone footbridge over a brook to continue past woodland (Bibsworth Covert) on your right.

Maintain your direction over a small wooden footbridge and a waymarked stile in the next corner. Cross a field to take a gate in the hedge on your right. Turn left to continue through a wooden gate. Go ahead along a lane past a conference centre on your left and through a security barrier. Go ahead across a road (Campden Lane) and take the stile beside a gate and a signpost opposite.

Bear right through an orchard to a stile. Maintain your general direction across a field to a waymark post on an old hedge line. Aim just to the left of the spire of Saintbury Church ahead. Reach a fence on your left and continue beside it to a stile in the corner. Cross it to reach a waymark post and bear left to, walk past the church on your right. Follow the path down to the road running through the village of Saintbury.

Go left through the village to the cross, beside the B4632 (until recently the A46 between Cheltenham and Stratford-upon-Avon). Retrace your steps to the waymark post below the church and go left to pass through the churchyard. Continue through a waymarked gate in the far wall of the churchyard.

Cross the neck of a field to a stile in the opposite fence. Bear right to climb through woodland to a waymarked stile in the top fence. Go ahead beside a hedge on your left. Notice the round barrow in the field on your right. Continue as waymarked, bearing left when you have almost reached the end of the field to join the road ahead (Campden Lane) through an old stone stile.

Cross the road with care and take the signposted bridleway opposite. There is woodland on your left and a fence on your right. Continue with a golf course on your left. Follow the track as it bends left to a waymarked gate on your right, which must be near the hermit's cell. This is also the modern county boundary.

Bear right downhill into Worcestershire and cross an estate road as shown by waymark posts. Continue downhill, with Broadway below you. Go through a gate in a fence and veer left, as waymarked. Walk around woodland on your left and follow a fence protecting newly-planted trees on your right. Go ahead through a waymarked hunting gate and veer right along a well-trodden path. This reaches a small waymarked gate near the end of the fence that is below on your right.

Pass through the gate and bear left to retrace your outward path through the gap in the hedge and across a field to a small, white, wooden gate. Go right to the footbridge for the enclosed path back to Broadway and its pubs.

2. CHIPPING CAMPDEN

Route: Chipping Campden – Dover's Hill – Ryknild Street – Kiftsgate Stone – Chipping Campden

Distance: 5$^1/_2$ miles

Map: O.S. Pathfinder 1043 Broadway & Chipping Campden

Start: The Volunteer Inn, Chipping Campden (Grid Reference: SP148389)

Access: Chipping Campden is at the junction of the B4035 and the B4081. It is possible, but not easy, to reach by public transport. Things would be a lot easier if British Rail would bow to local demand (and that of Cotswold Wayfarers) and reopen the station on its line between Oxford and Worcester. There is an assortment of local buses to various places at infrequent intervals. These are usually geared to school hours, and include a link with British Rail stations at both Moreton-in-Marsh and Evesham. The services are run by Barry's Coaches (tel. 0608 50876).

The Volunteer Inn (0386 840688)

Old military helmets adorn the walls of this pub with a difference. It got its name when volunteers signed on here in the 19th century. They spent their Queen's shillings before finding themselves destined for India or other parts of the Empire. Some were used to quell civil disturbances at home. A record of volunteers' names is kept in the pub, so family tree enthusiasts also find their way here. Accommodation is available, as are bar snacks and meals. There is a beer garden and, of course, real ale (including the local Hook Norton). Cars should be parked in the High Street, where the buses also stop. Opening hours are 11.30 a.m. to 2.30 p.m. and 7 p.m. to 11 p.m. on weekdays, 12 noon to 3 p.m. and 7 p.m. to, 10.30 p.m. on Sundays.

Chipping Campden

This handsome country town is built of the characteristic sandy coloured stone. It grew up on an ancient drove route and was granted a market

The Volunteer, Chipping Campden

charter in 1180 – 'Chipping' is derived from the Saxon word 'ceping', meaning a market. Cotswold fleeces were in demand on the continent in the Middle Ages and the town became rich on the backs of the sheep. Merchants inspected and bought the raw fleeces in the 14th century building that now houses the Woolstaplers Hall Museum and the Tourist Information Centre. The most successful of them was William Grevel, on whom Geoffrey Chaucer based the merchant in Canterbury Tales. Grevel's house still stands, opposite the museum; the parish church contains what is claimed to be the largest memorial brass in the Cotswolds to him, 'the flower of the wool merchants of all England'.

As the export of raw wool declined in favour of cloth, however, the centre of the woollen trade shifted to Stroud, with its many watermills. This has preserved a fine old town here for tourists to appreciate. Many now come with walking boots and rucksacks. The Market Hall (built in 1627) is the official start of the Cotswold Way. A better plan would be to walk north (up the maps) from Bath and finish here, preferably at St James' Church, which is a splendid example of a 'wool church'. Approaching the church along Leysbourne brings a view of the Ernest

Wilson Memorial Garden. This commemorates the great plant collector who was born here in 1876 and often visited the Far East. Returning along Church Street brings you past a row of almshouses built in 1612.

The Old Market Hall, Chipping Campden

Dover's Hill

There are memorable views over the Vale of Evesham, of Bredon Hill and towards the Malverns, from this delightful spot. Come here on a Spring Bank Holiday Monday to see the traditional games. These were inaugurated at Whitsuntide in 1612 by Captain Robert Dover from whom the hill takes its name. An eccentric and wealthy lawyer, he opened an 'Olimpick Games' on horseback wearing a suit supplied by King James I and wearing a feathered hat. Events included leap-frogging, wrestling, skittles, tilting the quintain, shinkicking and singlestick fighting (where the aim was to break your opponent's head).

Apart from a break enforced by hostilities during the Civil War period (when one of the last battles of the conflict was fought on the slopes of the hill), these games were held annually until 1852. Up to 30,000 attended in the early 19th century and the arrival of workers constructing the railway between Oxford and Worcester led to outbreaks of hooliganism. This gave the excuse to enclose the land and prevent further games. Exclusion was followed by the threat of development in the 1920s. The artist and architect F.L. Griggs fought hard to prevent this and to acquire the site for the public. He won and established the Campden Trust in 1929. The annual games were revived in 1951 and the site is now in the care of the National Trust. A topograph near the car park serves as a memorial to F.L. Griggs.

The Kiftsgate Stone

This is a holed stone about three feet in height, standing beside the road at the edge of the wood. It is an ancient 'moot' point. Kifts comes from 'cyft' (old English) meaning meeting or conference. Gate comes from 'geat', the Saxon word for a track. Local and national announcements were made here, including the reading of Magna Carta and the proclamations of coronations up to William IV's.

The Walk

With your back to The Volunteer, go ahead up the lane signposted as the Cotswold Way. This continues as Hoo Lane. Its surface deteriorates as it rises, waymarked as the Cotswold Way, to Kingcomb Lane.

Turn left along the road for about 75 yards, then turn right to follow the signposted Cotswold Way towards Dover's Hill. Walk beside a hedge on your right and continue over a stile in the corner. Turn left and walk towards the edge of the hill to enjoy the view. Keep parallel to the hedge on your left. Pass a stile in the corner of a fence on your left and continue with a line of trees on your left to a car park (the topograph is on your right).

Go down to a road and depart, temporarily, from the Cotswold Way by turning right. This means going down a 14% (or 1 in 7) gradient. As you approach trees on your right, look out for a signpost and a stile on your left.

Turn left over the stile to follow the signposted path. Walk with a hedge on your left and superb views on your right. Reach a gate on your left

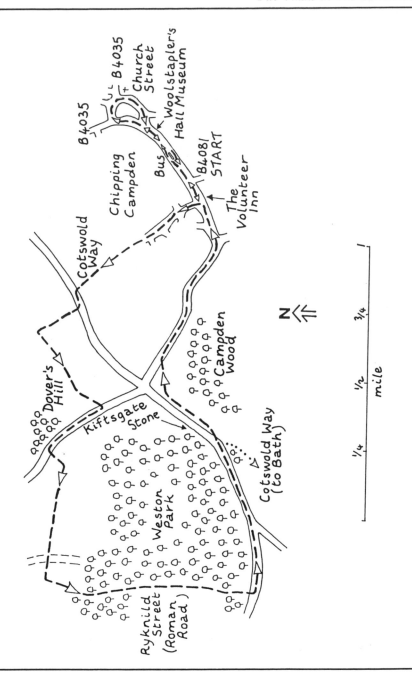

and bear right downhill to a waymarked stile in the bottom fence. Continue descending to another waymarked stile in a lower fence. Keep descending to cross a track at the signposted point.

Continue to a footbridge over a stream in the far left corner of the field. This is the first of two footbridges (go left – ignore the one ahead). Cross the subsequent stile and follow a brook on your right for 100 yards before veering left to a waymarked stile in an indented corner.

Cross the stile and a footbridge over a stream, then turn left along a muddy woodland track. This climbs to keep beside the stream on your left. Emerge through a waymarked gate to follow the old Roman road known as Ryknild Street. This follows the edge of fields, keeping beside the perimeter fence Of the wood on your left.

Go ahead through a gate in the corner leading back 'into the wood. Follow the muddy track up to a road and turn left along it. Go ahead at a junction, towards Chipping Campden.

The trees of Weston Park are constant companions on your left. Look out for a small triangle of trees on your right. Just after this is a Cotswold Way signpost. You can leave the road by going ahead along the Cotswold Way parallel to it, on your left. Don't miss the Kiftsgate Stone on the edge on the wood across the road on your left, after about 200 yards.

Walking along the headland path parallel to the road, look out for a gate on the left-hand side of the road. This marks where you leave the Cotswold Way again by bearing right down the field along a well-trodden path. Reach a signpost at the side of Dyers Lane and turn right along this road back to Chipping Campden. Fork left along Park Road to the Volunteer, on your right.

Extend this walk by going up Chipping Campden's High Street. Go to the left of the Market Hall, pass the Woolstaplers Hall Museum (incorporating the Tourist Information Centre) on your right and Grevel's 14th century house opposite it, on your left. Go ahead along Leysbourne to see the Ernest Wilson Memorial Garden in the lower half of the old vicarage garden on your right. Turn right along Cidermill Lane to the parish church dedicated to St James and take Church Street, passing the old almshouses on your right, back to the High Street. Go left to return to The Volunteer.

3.SNOWSHILL

Route: Snowshill – Great Brockhamton Farm – Broadway – Broadway Tower – Seven Wells Farm – Snowshill

Distance: $8^1/_2$ miles

Map: O.S. Pathfinder 1043 Broadway & Chipping Campden

Start: Snowshill Arms (Grid Reference: SP096337)

Access: Snowshill is about three miles south of Broadway. If you take the road between the two, you will find a car park on the edge of Snowshill, at the northern end of the village. Patrons can also park at the Snowshill Arms. If you rely on public transport, join this walk halfway round at Broadway. There are buses to Broadway from Cheltenham and Evesham, where there are British Rail stations. Telephone Castleways on 0242 602949/603715 for details.

Snowshill Arms (0386 852653)

There can be few more attractive and beautifully situated pubs. It is a 17th century building with an extension dating from the start of the 20th century. The interior features a partly-panelled open-plan beamed bar, while some stripped stone walls can be seen. The furnishings are appropriately simple, with wall-benches, pine tables and seats on a carpeted floor. There is a play area for children in the garden. Donnington Real Ale is served, as are meals, snacks and morning coffee. The local spring water was once used to brew whisky, while the Beard family that used to own the pub also brewed their own-label ginger beer. The opening hours are 11.30 a.m. to 2.30 p.m. and 6.30 p.m. to 11 p.m. Mondays to Fridays; 11 a.m. to 2.30 p.m. and 6.30 p.m. to 11 p.m. on Saturdays; and 12 noon to 2.30 p.m. and 7 p.m. to 10.30 p.m. on Sundays.

Snowshill

One of the last of the great eccentrics turned Snowshill's historic manor house into a collector's treasure chest. Charles Paget Wade filled the main building with English, European and Oriental furniture, craft tools, toys, clocks, bicycles and musical instruments. He was forced to move into the Priest's House in the grounds, but began to fill that up too. Refusing modern amenities and sleeping in a Tudor cupboard-bed, he eventually married and retired to the West Indies, where an estate was the source of his wealth. He died there in 1956, five years after giving Snowshill Manor to the National Trust. The 16th century manor house was once owned by Catherine Parr, the sixth and last of Henry VIII's wives. Now, it is open to the public from Wednesday to Saturday (and Bank Holiday Mondays) between May and September, also weekends in April and October. The displays include one of Japanese Samurai armour.

The church at Snowshill

Broadway

This is now a showpiece much visited by Americas tourists, having been 'discovered' by William Morris. Its name reflects the width of the High Street, which used to form part of the stage-coach route between London and Worcester. It is a really beautiful mile-long example of Cotswold stone building.

Broadway Tower

This is built on an ancient beacon site. It is also on the curiously-named Fish Hill. Is this a reference to Pisces in a terrestrial zodiac? The tower was completed in 1798 from a design by James Wyatt as a folly for the Earl of Coventry's Springhill estate. It was reputedly built as a signalling tower to the family estate at Croone Court, some 15 miles away to the south of Worcester.

William Morris spent holidays here and must have enjoyed the view from 1024 ft, the second-highest spot on the Cotswolds. There is a topograph to help you identify the Black Mountains, the Malverns and the Wrekin. Twelve counties can be seen from here. The tower is now the centre-piece of a Country Park, for which there is an admission charge. This route sticks to the rights of way, which are free and open all year, unlike the Country Park, which is open between April and September.

Seven Wells Farm

This curious place, with its ring of trees, features on the ley described going through Saintbury in Walk 1. There were wells here long before the farm buildings were erected. Historian and novelist Hugh Ross set his story of 'The Silver Bowl' (1948) here. The novel's title is a reference to a reputedly real find in the semicircle of trees that now shield the farm. The place is associated with witches.

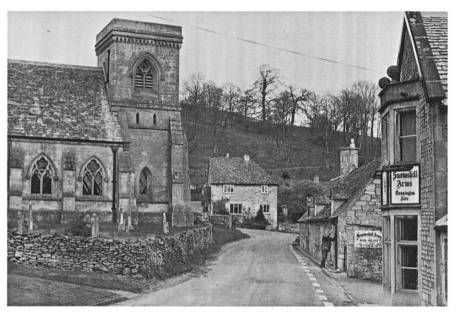

The Snowshill Arms

The Walk

With your back to the Snowshill Arms, go right (to pass the church on your left) and bear right along the road past Oat House on your left. Bear right immediately after this, going through a gate to follow a descending track.

Continue through a gate across the track and walk beside a fence on your right. Approach a lower gate and leave the track just before it. Continue with a fence on your right, overlooking a lake on your right that is so new that it isn't marked on the maps yet. Turn right over a stile in the corner and go left along a fenced path. Cross a waymarked stile to the right of a wooden gate at its end.

Follow the well-trodden path up the valley, heading for a gate in a fence to the left of Great Brockhamton Farm. Turn left after the gate and, after 100 yards, double back along the metalled lane going right to pass above the farm on your right.

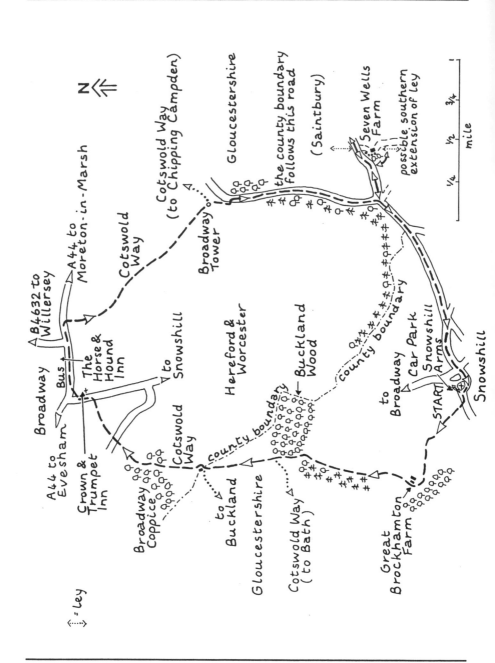

Continue along the lane past a ladder stile beside a footpath signpost on your right. Walk with a forest on your left as the lane deteriorates to a track. Continue through a gate ahead and go down to a Cotswold Way signpost. Go ahead along the track, ignoring signposted stiles on your right. You are now following the Cotswold Way.

Just before the track bends left down to Buckland, turn right as directed by a Cotswold Way signpost. Follow a fence on your right to a stile beside a gate. Go over this and turn left, as waymarked, to follow the fence on your left. Continue over a stile to the left of a gate ahead. Cross the following stile beside a gate to go ahead with a hedge on your right.

Take the waymarked wooden gate in the next corner and bear right down a path through Broadway Copse. This curves left, then forks right (as waymarked) down to a wooden gate in the lower perimeter fence. Go downhill to a stile in the bottom corner. Follow an enclosed path to a road.

Cross the road to take the waymarked Cotswold Way opposite. Walk towards the church, crossing a field, a footbridge and a stile. Continue through a kissing-gate to a lane which takes you to Broadway's Church Street. Go left to pass St Michael's Church on your right and past the Crown & Trumpet Inn on your right. Turn right along Broadway's High Street.

Reach a Cotswold Way signpost and turn right, away from the High Street. Follow a walled track to a stile beside a gate. Cross a yard to another stile beside a gate and go ahead down a field to cross a bridge over a stream. Go up to a stile beside a gate in the far corner. Bear half left from this to the next gateway. Veer slightly right to a waymark post in the next field and continue to a gate in the far right corner.

Cross a waymarked stile beside a gate and follow a gradual climb beside a wall on your left. Go straight up along this path to Broadway Tower. Bear right, away from the Cotswold Way, along the ridge of Fish Hill along the public footpath (stray and pay!) to a stile this side of the entrance to the country park. Cross the stile and turn left to reach a road.

Turn right along the road. Pass the access track to Heath Farm on your left. Divert left along a minor road signposted to Chipping Campden.

This is in order to see Seven Wells Farm, on the line of the ley which features on the Saintbury walk (no 1). If you have your dowsing rods, go along the road to pick up the ley at the end of the wall and the trees on your right. Explore, too, the signposted path which takes you round the semicircle of trees which shelter the farm. A ladder stile leads to a field. Keep the wall on your left and reach the ley, which is going roughly north-south, before the footpath reaches a farm track. Retrace your steps to the road junction and go ahead along the signposted road to Snowshill.

Reach a crossroads at the edge of Snowshill. Go ahead, downhill, and follow the road as it bends right. Go through the churchyard to reach the Snowshill Arms.

4. STANWAY HOUSE

Route: Stanton – Laverton Hill – Lidcombe Wood – Stanway House – Stanton

Distance: $6^1/_2$ miles

Map: O.S. Pathfinder 1043 Broadway & Chipping Campden

Start: The Mount Inn, Stanton (Grid Reference: SP072342)

Access: Go through the village of Stanton , just off the B4632, to reach the Mount Inn, which has a car park for patrons. Some buses on Castleway's service between Cheltenham and Broadway enter the village, while others pass within one mile (tel. 0242 602949/603715 for details).

The Mount Inn (0386 73316)

This is a 'chip free' zone! There is an extensive menu, with 'cow pie' the local speciality. You can join in a game of 'boules' in the summer, while the pub also has its own cricket team, known as the MCC. When Rachel Heyhoe-Flint was denied access to the Long Room at Lord's, this MCC promptly honoured her with membership of their club. Indoor games feature in the winter, when there is a quiz night on alternate Thursdays. Oh, yes, they also serve Donningtons Real Ale. A real log fire enhances winter evenings, while children are welcome in the beer garden in the summer. The building dates from at least 1610 and is open from 11 a.m. to 3 p.m. and 6 p.m. to 11 p.m. Mondays to Fridays; 11 a.m. through to 11 p.m. on Saturdays; 12 noon to 3 p.m. and 7 p.m. to 10.30 p.m. on Sundays.

Stanton

This village is a chocolate box picture. Is it a village or a folk museum? Farm workers and children appear to be scarce, but the pub has plenty of life in it. This is a tidy place, being a regular winner of Gloucestershire's best-kept village title. Many of the buildings date from

The Mount Inn and Stanton Village

about 1600 and were restored in the early 20th century by the architect Sir Phillip Stott, who lived here. They are fine examples of the golden Cotswold limestone hewn from local quarries. Even post second world war council houses conform to the traditional Cotswold building style. The church contains remains of early 14th century wall paintings. The young John Wesley is reputed to have delivered his first sermon here. He liked to visit his friends, the sons and daughters of the Rev. Lionel Kirkham. Some of the pew-ends in St Michael's Church bear gouge marks made by the ropes used to attach the sheepdogs which accompanied the shepherds to services.

Stanway House

This is a handsome Jacobean manor house filled with splendid furniture and sat in delightful grounds. This walk passes the gatehouse, which was the work of Timothy Strong of Taynton and not, as once thought, of Inigo Jones. Dr Thomas Dover, the grandson of the man who started the games at Dover's Hill near Chipping Campden, once lived here. He was the person who rescued Alexander Selkirk, the model for Robinson Crusoe, from the island of Juan Fernandez in 1708. Still privately owned, the manor is usually open to the public on Tuesdays and Thursdays, June to August (tel. 0386 73469).

The Walk

Go downhill from the pub and along the village street. Turn right at a telephone box to follow a track to a waymarked stile beside a gate. Continue walking parallel to a fence on your right. Go through a waymarked gate in the next corner and walk beside a hedge on your left. Cross a stile in the hedge ahead. Continue veering slightly right along a well-trodden path to a waymarked gap in the next hedge. Go ahead to a stile which precedes a footbridge over a brook. Continue across the corner of the next field to a stile in the fence ahead. Maintain your direction up a long field to a small wooden gate in the far fence.

Cross a field to a waymarked stile in a fence. Walk through a belt of trees to emerge at a willow-lined brook. Cross this, but soon turn right up an old green lane. This goes through a gate and climbs gradually along a sunken track which is joined by a fence on your right. Go through a gate in the top corner near a Cotswold Way signpost. Turn

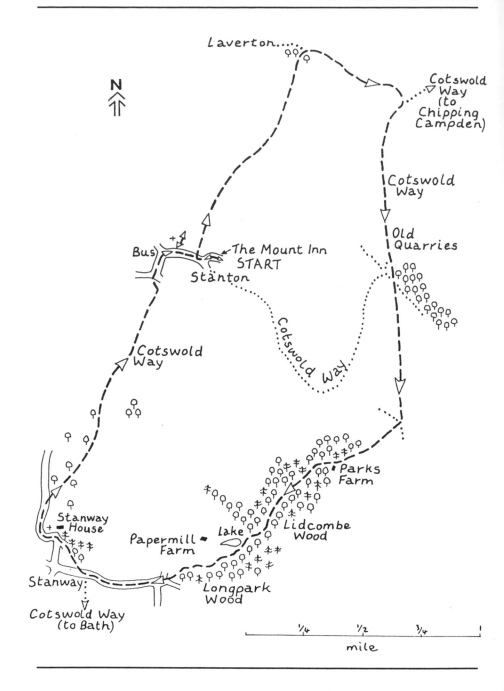

right along the fenced track of the Cotswold Way, which is here waymarked with red arrows plus the distinctive white dot of the Way. Continue to a signpost marking where the Cotswold Way turns sharply right over a cattle grid.

Leave the Cotswold Way, for a while, by going ahead along the track with a fence on your left. Very soon fork right from this, at the start of woodland on your left. Take a blue waymarked gate into a field and walk beside a fence on your right.

Continue through a waymarked gate and with a wall on your right. Go ahead through two more gates, still beside a wall on your right. Don't be tempted by a waymarked stile in a corner formed by a wall and a fence ahead, on your left. Ignore also a waymarked gate in the wall on your right, but do bear right through a small, waymarked, metal gate immediately after it.

Cut across a field diagonally to a small metal gate in the fence opposite. Maintain your direction over the next field to a small wooden gate in a wall. Pass a yellow-arrowed stile into woodland on your right but veer right ahead as waymarked by a blue arrow.

Follow a track past the perimeter wall of the woodland on your right. Do not take a yellow-arrowed gate bearing right into this wood, but do go ahead down the blue-arrowed track which enters the wood through a gate ahead.

Green-topped wooden posts augmented by blue arrows show the way through Lidcombe Wood. Keep to the waymarked bridleway to follow a wall on your right (this soon becomes a fence). Pass above Papermill Farm with its lake in the valley on your right. Emerge between cottages on a lane and go right down to a road.

Go right to follow the pavement into Stanway. Pass a Cotswold Way signpost on your left, then bear right over a stile beside a gate to follow the north-bound Cotswold Way which is signposted to Stanton. Veer right at a waymark post, turn left to walk with a wall on your left and take a kissing gate ahead. Follow a walled path to a signpost.

Bear right along a lane and go right, as waymarked, at a T-junction. Pass the gatehouse of Stanway House and St Peter's Church on your right.

Stanway House Gate

Follow the road as it turns right and bear right from it when you come to a stile beside a Cotswold Way signpost.

Cut across a corner to a stile in an iron fence. Go ahead as waymarked to cross parkland to another stile. Bear left to a waymarked gate and continue to a stile in a hedge. This is followed by a footbridge and another stile. A well-trodden fieldpath (this is a popular section of the Cotswold Way) leads to a stile in the next hedge. Continue beside a hedge on your right.

Cross a stile in the next corner and go ahead over the following field to a stile beside a Cotswold Way signpost. This leads to a lane which you turn left down to reach a road. Go right (but ignore a No Through Road on your extreme right) and turn right at the war memorial to walk through Stanton. Divert left at the old cross to visit St Michael's Church. Continue up the street and back to the Mount Inn, Stanton.

5. MORETON-IN-MARSH

Route: The Black Bear Inn, Moreton-in-Marsh – Batsford – The Horse and Groom Inn, Bourton-on-the-Hill – Sezincote House – The Black Bear Inn, Moreton-in-Marsh

Distance: 9 miles

Maps: O.S. Pathfinders 1043 Broadway and 1044 Moreton-in-Marsh

Start: The Black Bear Inn (Grid Reference: SP205325)

Access: Moreton-in-Marsh has a station on the British Rail line between Oxford and Worcester. Take the station access drive on your left and turn right up New Road past the Post Office on your right. This brings you to the broad High Street. The Black Bear Inn is on this side of the road on your left, near the Town Hall in the centre of the street. This is the A429 on the line of the Roman Fosse Way from Cirencester to Halford, where the A429 diverges from the Fosse Way towards Leamington. Cars can be parked in the centre of the High Street outside the Black Bear Inn. Local buses stop near the Town Hall. Telephone 0452 425543 for the latest information on these varied but infrequent services. There is, for example, a summer service (no. X37) on Tuesdays only from Stroud. Also, several Barry's Coaches from Chipping Campden and a daily service from Cheltenham on Pulham's Coaches, who also run a bus (P17) on Tuesdays only from Witney.

The Black Bear Inn (0608 50705)

You can stay here on a bed and breakfast basis. Try room 4 and see if you smell perfume. This could be Fred the ghost. He turns taps off too. It's hard to say how old Fred is, but parts of the building date back to the 17th century, when there was a priest's hole. Food and real ale are served, including Donningtons, from a small brewery in Stow-on-the-Wold. Opening hours are 11 a.m. to 3 p.m. (4 p.m. on Market Day, Tuesday) and 6 p.m. to 11 p.m. during the week. Noon to 3 p.m. and 7 p.m. to 10.30 p.m. on Sundays.

The Black Bear

The Horse and Groom (0386 700413)

It's always useful to know about emergency watering-holes halfway
around the course. This one is at Bourton-on-the-Hill and serves real ale
(Bass). There is a beer garden, food, and bed and breakfast accommodation too in this 17th century pub. The landlord assures me there are no
ghosts.

The Fosse Way

This Roman road runs straight through Moreton-in-Marsh on its way
between Exeter and Lincoln, a total distance of 182 miles. Don't try to
walk it all unless you like car fumes and busy roads. This was the initial
boundary of Roman Britain, created around 47 AD before the legions
dared to push on to the wilder north and west. Some say it still divides
the nation between soft and hard, rich and poor. As its original purpose
was mainly military, there must have been forts and camps at regular
intervals. There was a Roman settlement just to the north of modern
Moreton-in-Marsh.

Moreton-in-Marsh

A natural route-centre, Moreton is on the way from Oxford to Worcester as well as on the Fosse Way. When the railway age came, it was the link between London and the cathedral cities of Oxford, Worcester and Hereford that proved to be vital. British Rail were still running a 'Cathedrals Express' between London and Hereford along this line in April, 1992. The Oxford, Worcester and Wolverhampton Railway (OW & W) was promoted by the Great Western Railway. Brunel was its chief Engineer and he started off by underestimating the price by 150% (£1 million became £2.5 million). It was important to the GWR as a route to the industrial west Midlands. Work started in 1845 but wasn't completed until 1853. Never famous for a fast service, it was familiarly known as the Old Worse and Worse. Today it is an attractive line through the Cotswolds which provides a service for commuters to Oxford, Worcester and London. It deserves to be better-promoted and used. A Sunday morning Ramblers' service would be one idea.

Batsford

If you have the time, do make a short diversion to this little estate village, with its 'mock' Norman church, complete with a tall spire. The fifty acres of woodland comprising Batsford Park Arboretum are the chief attraction, however. Scenic walks afford fine views over the Evenlode valley and into Oxfordshire. Over one thousand different trees, bamboos and shrubs have been assembled from such exotic places as

Japan, China, Nepal and North America. The arboretum was created by
Bertie Mitford, the first Lord Redesdale and a traveller and diplomat, in
the 1880s. There is a teashop open from Easter to October (tel. 0386
700409 for more details).

Bourton-on-the-Hill

Less visited than its watery namesake, this could be as perfect a
Cotswold village – if it wasn't for the noisy A44 running through it. It
was once owned by the abbots of Westminster, who found the income
provided by the wool from the local sheep very useful. Some of it was
spent glorifying the parish church (St Lawrence's), which dates from
Norman times. This Bourton is a proud past winner of the Bledisloe Cup
for the 'Best Kept Village'.

Sezincote

Here stands a piece of oriental splendour on a Cotswold hillside. The old
estate was purchased by Colonel John Cockerell in 1795, upon his return
from Bengal. It was inherited by his younger brother, Charles, who had
also served in the East India Company and who built a new house here.

The architect was a third brother, Samuel Pepys Cockerell (the brothers
were related to the famous diarist). He was a surveyor to the East India
Company and worked closely with Thomas Daniel, an artist who was
also home from India. The design of his house was inspired by the
works of Akbar, the 16th century Mogul emperor. The landscape artist,
Humphrey Repton, enhanced it by turning the River Evenlode into
water gardens and lakes on the hillside below the house (and where the
footpath passes). The interior is as unique (telephone 0386 700444 for
details of visits). When the Prince Regent visited Sezincote in 1806, he
was won over to the design and ordered his Pavilion at Brighton to be
based on it. John Nash was the prince's architect, rather than Cockerell,
however.

The Walk

Carefully cross the High Street from the Black Bear Inn and take Corders
Lane ahead. Cross Hospital Road at a T-junction and go ahead along a

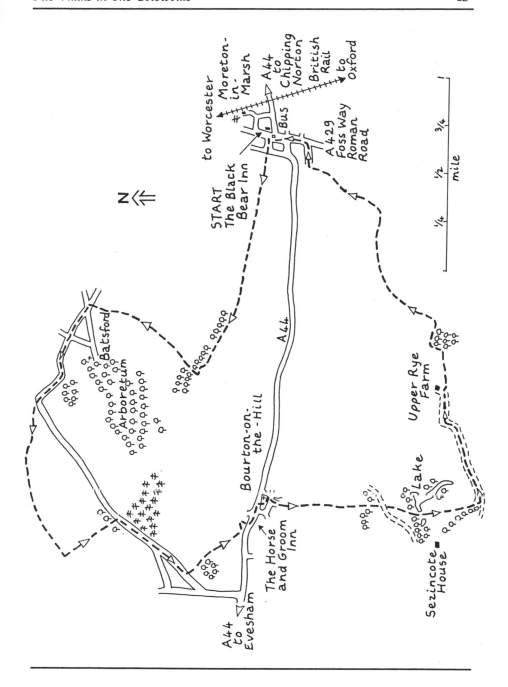

signposted enclosed path. Emerge through a kissing-gate onto a field. Go ahead to cross a stile in the fence on your left. Bear right across the corner of the next field to a waymarked metal kissing-gate.

Maintain your direction across the next field to a stile beside a kissing-gate. Cross another field to a stile and continue over its field to another waymarked kissing-gate. Go ahead to a kissing-gate beside a gate in the far right corner of this field, near a copse.

Veer right to walk as waymarked beside a fence and trees on your right. Cross a small stone slab footbridge over a brook. Continue over a waymarked stile beside a gate in the far corner of the field. At the next corner, turn right over a waymarked stile to take a path through trees and back over another stile to the field that was ahead of you.

Turn right when you are in the field and reach a signpost. Turn right through a small wooden gate to reach the corner of the field on the other side of the trees. Walk with a wall on your left past three fields. Continue over a stile beside a gate to enter parkland and walk with a fence on your right.

Go ahead over a stile to the left of a gate in the corner ahead and walk with a fence now on your left. Turn left over the next stile and then right immediately to cross another stile. Follow the fenced path, crossing yet another stile and walking between newly planted trees to reach a road.

Turn left and walk uphill over two crossroads (unless you wish to divert to Batsford, on your left). Reach a corner where the road turns left and take the fieldgate ahead to bear left along a signposted bridleway. This continues through a small wooden gate in the far left corner. Go through it to walk with a fence on your right.

Ignore the waymarked wooden fieldgate on your right and take the small wooden gate in the corner ahead to follow an enclosed ridge path. The blue arrowed bridleway which forks right to run parallel with this path before descending to Blockley is not for you! Stay on the fine ridge path with views over Blockley on your right until a gate across the path ahead.

Turn left immediately before the gate across the ridge path and go through a small, waymarked gate. Walk beside a wall and a row of trees on your right and go ahead over a stile beside a gate to reach a road.

Go right along the road and keep left, or straight on, when the road forks. Reach a fieldgate waymarked with a blue arrow on your left. Turn left through it and follow the fence on your left. Ignore a track into woodland on your right. Go ahead along a track which has a hedge on your left and a fence on your right.

Reach a gate, go through it and turn left towards a farm along an access track. Turn right before the buildings to pass a waymarked vehicle barrier and reach the A44 road. Go left into Bourton-on-the-Hill and seek refuge from the traffic in the Horse and Groom, across the road on your right.

Continue down to the parish church and follow the path through the churchyard. Go right when you emerge at a road, then turn right at a crossroads near a telephone box. After 50 yards, turn left along the signposted path to Sezincote. This begins as a walled track.

Emerge through a waymarked gate into the corner of a field. Continue beside a wall on your right down to another gate. Maintain this direction across the next field to a gate in the hedge ahead. Go through and walk with a hedge on your left and veer very slightly right to a stile in a wooden fence ahead.

Go ahead across the next field as waymarked by an arrow on a log. Take a kissing-gate to a short path between trees to a second waymarked kissing-gate. Walk ahead to cross a drive and follow the direction of the waymark on a second recumbent log. Descend to a gate, walk between the lake on your left and the water gardens on your right to emerge through a second gate onto more parkland.

Look right for a view of Sezincote House. Continue through a gate in the fence ahead and climb to the far top right corner. A kissing-gate beside a gate leads to a farm road, near a cattle grid. Go left down it until the road turns left into a farmyard (Upper Rye Farm).

Follow the yellow waymark arrows to go straight ahead, passing the farm on your left. Go through a gate, ignore a waymarked path on your left and keep to the right of barns ahead. Walk over the next field towards a copse. Turn left to pass the copse on your right, continue through a waymarked gate and turn right in the next field.

Go ahead about 200 yards to a path junction in the middle of the field that is marked only by the paths trodden in the grass. Turn left to reach a gate. Go ahead, as waymarked, to walk with a hedge on your right. Continue through a gate in the next corner and follow the direction of the waymark arrow to gradually converge with the hedge on your left in the next field. Take the gate in the corner ahead, ignore a muddy track to the farm on your left but cross a stile to the left of a gate ahead. Follow the hedge on your left and go through a waymarked gate in the next corner to keep beside it until you reach a signpost between two gates.

Turn left through the second of the two gates and walk with the hedge on your left to a gate in the corner. Go ahead through it to follow an old green lane, past the backs of houses on your right. Turn right to pass fire and ambulance stations, followed by a duck pond. Reach the Fosse Way and turn left along it back to the High Street, Moreton-in-Marsh. Notice the old wooden stocks on the green before Market Hall. The Black Bear Inn is just after the Market Hall, across the road on your right.

6. WINCHCOMBE AND BELAS KNAP

Route: WInchcombe – Corndean Lane – Hill Barn Farm – Belas Knap – Wadfield Farm – Sudeley Castle – Winchcombe

Distance: 7 miles

Map: O.S. Pathfinder 1067 Winchcombe and Stow-on-the-Wold

Start: The Old Corner Cupboard Inn, Winchcombe (Grid Reference: SP021282)

Access: The Old Corner Cupboard Inn stands in Gloucester Street, which is the B4632 at the western end of Winchcombe. There is a car park at the back, down Malthouse Lane. Conveniently, there is a bus stop outside. Buses also stop at Abbey Terrace. The chief service is provided by Castleways, the 1989 National Award Winner of 'Best Bus Company in Britain' (tel. 0242 602949/603715). There is a good service to and from Cheltenham (including Sunday afternoons) and on weekdays buses link at Willersey for Evesham (on British Rail).

The Old Corner Cupboard Inn (0242 602303)

Winchcombe exudes history, so it seems appropriate to start from a building which dates back to at least 1550. Its iole was that of a farmhouse until the 19th century, however. A bust of Disraeli can be seen above the door. More elusive is the ghost of a mysterious 12 year old girl, usually seen wearing a white dress and apparently friendly. A new licensee is expected in June 1992, but opening times should remain at 11.30 a.m. to 2.30 p.m. and 5.30 p.m. to 11 p.m. Real ales are served, including Flowers. Food is available and there is a beer garden. A self-catering unit is available on a weekly and seasonal basis. One thing that ramblers are asked to remember is to take their boots off!

Winchcombe

Nestling in a fold of the Cotswolds, Winchcombe can testify to a surprising history. The Romans were here, perhaps nearly three thousand years after the builders of Belas Knap. Fame came in Saxon times, when the town was the capital of the Hwicce, a sub-kingdom within Mercia. King Offa (well-known for building the dyke on the Welsh frontier) founded a nunnery here in 787. King Kenulf or Caenwulf, established an abbey here in 811, dedicated by the Archbishop of Canterbury. Kenulf had a palace here and was buried in the abbey in 821. The Danes sacked the place but the abbey was refounded by the Benedictines in 969. 'Wincelcumbe' was the capital of its own shire in the 11th century and was defended by stout ramparts.

A regular influx of pilgrims to the shrine of St Kenelm, a murdered boy prince, swelled the coffers of a market town. It also benefited from the wool trade in the Middle Ages. St Peter's parish church was built in the 1460s in the perpendicular style and adorned with gargoyles. It came in time, for the abbey was destroyed at the Dissolution. This came as a blow to the local economy and desperation led to enterprise.

Tobacco was grown here in the 17th century in defiance of governments committed to protecting the colonial trade.

The town went into a decline only arrested in the late 20th century when its peaceful situation attracted the newly-retired and the newly-mobile workers of the motor-car age. Proof of a rowdier past is provided by the wooden stocks kept under the old Town Hall, now the Tourist Information Centre and the Folk and Police Museums. There are holes for seven legs, prompting a legend of a notorious one-legged offender. The width of Abbey Terrace allowed for an annual Mop Fair, when women seeking domestic employment went on display. No 23 Gloucester Street houses a small Railway Museum. This is packed with interest and is well worth a visit (Easter – October, daily 1.30 – 6 p.m. and winter weekends 1.30 – dusk, tel. 0242 – 602257/626410). Winchcombe lost its station in 1962, but enthusiasts are relaying the track between Cheltenham Racecourse and Stratford Racecourse.

Sudeley Castle

The public now flocks to the castle's gardens and the specialist garden centre, while there is a magnificent adventure playground complete with a wooden castle. Privately owned, the castle is opened daily except in the winter. A royal estate in the ninth century, it belonged to Ralph Boteler, Baron Sudeley, in the 15th century. Lost to the crown during the Wars of the Roses, it became a home to Henry VIII's wives. Both Catherine of Aragon and Anne Boleyn (wives one and two) came here. Wife six, Henry's widow Katherine Parr, is buried here, having married Thomas Seymour, who became Lord Sudeley. Cromwell knocked the place about more than his proverbial 'bit'. It became habitable again and then only in part, in the 19th century. Today it houses paintings by Rubens, Turner and Van Dyke.

Sudeley Castle

Belas Knap

Dating from about 2500 BC (New Stone Age), this is an impressive long barrow. There is a false entrance at the front formed by two upright stones with a lintel across the top and a stone blocking the centre. The width is 60 feet (reaching a height of 13 feet) at this northern end. The length is 180 feet and there are two burial chambers on the eastern side, one at the southern end and one on the western side. A total of 38 human skeletons has been found, while there is evidence of dry-stone walling having been practised in these parts for thousands of years. Wadfield Roman Villa, below Belas Knap, is on private land but marked by a plantation of trees. 'Wad' may refer to woad, used as a dye. Shortly after it is an elegant 18th century mansion.

The Walk

With your back to The Old Corner Cupboard Inn, go left to the Railway Museum. Cross the road carefully to take Mill Lane on your right. Descend to a Cycleway sign and bear right, with a hedge on your left and a wall on your right, to a footbridge across the River Isbourne. Go ahead over it to pass the dressing rooms of Winchcombe Town Football Club on your left. Continue through a wooden kissing-gate and bear right across pasture to a stone stile near a gate in the far corner.

Go left along a minor road (Corndean Lane) for a quarter of a mile. Just before the road narrows, bear right along a rough track which gives access to Corndean Hall and is signposted as the path to Belas Knap. Pass a cricket ground on your right. When the track veers right, go straight ahead to a stile.

Follow the signposted path up the pasture to a wooden step stile in the top fence. Continue climbing to a stone stile which gives access to Corndean Lane again. Go right along it, still climbing. Ignore a fork down towards Corndean Hall on your right. The lane passes through a plantation of conifer trees to reach Hill Barn Farm.

Maintain your direction along a rough track. Look out for a signpost at a junction and turn sharply left towards Belas Knap. Follow the edge of a field on your right, keeping near a wall on your left. A stone stile in the corner ahead leads to Belas Knap long barrow.

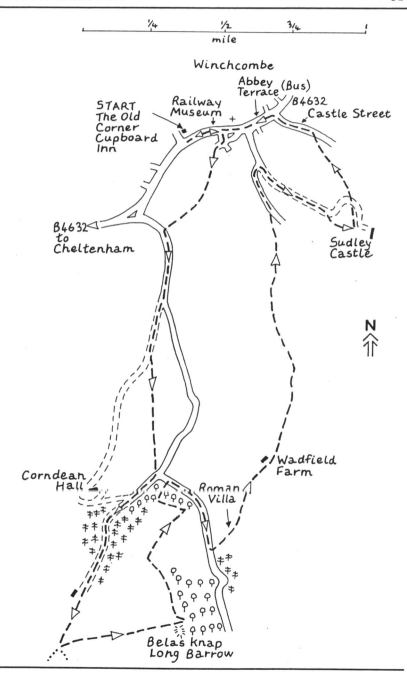

Pass the false entrance of the long barrow on your right. Cross a stone stile in the boundary wall to enter a belt of woodland. Turn left to go through a metal kissing-gate and follow a path which bends left. Go right as you emerge from the trees and follow the edge of a field on your left, with trees and a wall on your right.

Ignore a small wooden gate on your right when the woodland there ends. Continue with a wall on your right and bend right with it to reach a metal kissing-gate. Go through this and descend beside a wall on your right. At the bottom corner, go left to follow a fence on your right until you reach a waymarked metal kissing-gate in it. Turn right through it to go down a woodland path. This deposits you at a stile beside a gate. Cross the stile to reach a minor road. Go right along this for a quarter of a mile.

Reach a Cotswold Way signpost and turn sharply left down a track to Humblebee Cottages. Follow the track as it bears left and below the plantation of trees covering the site of Wadfield Roman Villa. Pass Wadfield Farm and its 18th century mansion on your left. Go ahead along a narrow, waymarked path, between fields (with a fence on your left and a hedgerow on your right).

Continue by crossing a wooden step stile ahead and descending with the hedge on your right. Ignore a metal fieldgate on your right and bear left beside a fence, as waymarked. Turn right over a stile and turn left immediately to follow a hedge on your left. Go around the bottom corner and turn left to cross a wooden footbridge and a subsequent stile into the next field.

Veer right to cross the field diagonally to a white markerboard. Go ahead over a stile into the next field and maintain this direction, as waymarked. Cross a stile in the next hedge and cross a field to a metal kissing-gate beside a fieldgate in the far corner. Go through to a lane and turn left along it for nearly 300 yards.

Turn sharply right at a signpost to enter the grounds of Sudeley Castle. Continue through a latch-gate to the left of a cattle grid. Follow the castle drive (waymarked as part of the Wardens Way) and resist the temptation to follow a grassy path signposted bearing left.

Bear right, as waymarked, through a metal gate at a second cattle grid. Pass the adventure playground on the other side of a fence on your left. Turn left through a kissing-gate beside a gate and pass the castle on your right. Keep beside a fence on your left to a stile ahead. Cross it and the subsequent metalled drive and another stile.

Maintain your direction, as waymarked, across a field to a kissing-gate beside a gate. Continue to the far corner of the next pasture, where a wooden kissing-gate leads to steps down to a road. Go left, back into Winchcombe (along Castle Street). Turn left at the High Street to pass the bus stops in Abbey Terrace and back down Gloucester Street to The Old Corner Cupboard Inn.

The Old Corner Cupboard Inn

7. NAUNTON

Route: Naunton – Windrush Way – Upper Slaughter – Wardens' Way – Naunton

Distance: $8^1/_2$ miles

Map: O.S. Pathfinder 1067 Winchcombe & Stow-on-the-Wold

Start: The Black Horse Inn, Naunton (Grid Reference: SP 119235)

Access: Naunton lies just north of the B4068 about four miles west-northwest of Bourton-on-the-Water. Patrons may park at the Black Horse Inn. If you come by bus, there are several infrequent services geared to villagers going out of Naunton to school or for shopping trips. The best service to visit Naunton from outside is Pulham's morning bus from Moreton-in-Marsh to Cheltenham, returning at lunch-time. Telephone Pulham's on 0451 20369 for full details. You may prefer to link this route with that from Bourton-on-the-Water at Upper Slaughter. This would give a full day of 15 miles but a better bus service connecting with trains at Moreton-in-Marsh.

The Black Horse Inn (0451 850378)

The building appears to have been two cottages which housed farm workers in the 17th century. Now its authentic beams are beautifully exposed in the tap room. This is a pleasant place to relax with good food and drink in peaceful surroundings. Accommodation is available. Opening hours are 11 a.m. to 2.30 p.m. and 6 p.m. to 11 p.m. on weekdays, 12 noon to 2 p.m. and 7p.m. to 10.30 p.m. on Sundays.

But is this all that can be said? Perhaps not. This may be a very special pub with a history linking us to the last Celtic Golden Age and the Knights of King Arthur. The clue is in the name. There aren't all that many Black Horse pubs in Britain. A map showing their distribution compares very well with a map showing the probable border zones between Britons and Saxons in the early sixth century. These would be the very areas patrolled by King Arthur's knights. They may have ridden black horses, as brought by the Romans to Hadrian's Wall. What would be more natural than to associate their watering-holes with the black horse? The Cotswolds, especially on this eastern side, were a border area. S. G. Wildman's book on the subject, 'The Black Horsemen' (John Baker, 1971), is thoroughly recommended. Before you leave, raise a glass to the men who rode the black horses.

Three Ways

Much of this walk follows two waymarked routes which link Winchcombe with Bourton-on-the-Water. These are the Wardens' Way and the Windrush Way. Although they are each only about 13^1/$_2$ miles long, they play an important role in the national network of long distance paths. Bourton-on-the-Water is one terminal point of the Oxfordshire Way despite being in Gloucestershire.

The Heart of England Way has also been recently extended to the town. This links with the Staffordshire Way, which links with the Gritstone Trail. This, in turn, connects with the Cestrian Link Walk which leads to Edale and the start of the Pennine Way (or Prestatyn and the Offa's Dyke Path). Scotland and Wales are at your feet! The Oxfordshire Way joins up with the Thames Path at Henley to take you to London. Winchcombe is just as vital a path junction, with the Cotswold Way passing through and the Wychavon Way terminating in the town.

The Wardens' Way is waymarked with two Ws (on top of each other white above green) and favours higher ground. Its name commemorates the Cotswold Voluntary Warden Service, which has done a sterling job in maintaining and waymarking the rights of way in this Area of Outstanding Natural Beauty.

The Windrush Way follows the valley of the river whose name it takes. Its waymark is a circle with a white top half and a green bottom half. The third 'Way' is the old, dismantled, railway, which can be seen from the Windrush Way. This was the Banbury and Cheltenham Direct Railway. This crossed the surviving Cotswold Line between Oxford and Worcester at Kingham (formerly known as Chipping Norton Junction). A branch line had reached Bourton-on-the Water by 1862, but the through-route opened in 1887. Dr Beeching took his scalpel to it in 1962. It used to take iron ore from Hook Norton to the coal of South Wales and cattle to market in Banbury. Expresses with through restaurant cars ran over its tracks on their way between Cardiff and Newcastle.

Upper Slaughter

It seems blood did not flow in the River Eye. The name may mean 'place of sloe trees' or 'muddy pools of water'. Some say it is derived from the d'Scholtres who built a Norman castle near the church, which is also Norman. There was a family called Slaughter living here in the 16th century. The manor house is Elizabethan and is open on Friday afternoons from May to September. The rector of St Peters' Church who died in 1854, F.E. Witts, had his diary published in 1979 – 'The Diary of a Cotswold Parson'.

Some cottages were restored in the early 20th century by the visionary architect Sir Edwin Lutyens. If you are lucky, you'll see a kingfisher in the valley of the River Eye.

The ford at Upper Slaughter

The Walk

With your back to the Black Horse Inn, go right towards the road junction and take the track on your left just before it. Cross the bridge over the River Windrush and take the gate ahead. Follow an enclosed path to a higher gate.

Continue with a wall on your right. Go ahead through a kissing-gate beside a fieldgate and walk past a second field on your left to reach a road (the B4068). Turn right along its grass verge. Reach a public bridleway signpost on your left and turn left through a gate to follow it. Descend with a wall on your left and ignore the track going left to a farm building.

Cross a stile beside a gate in the corner ahead and bear left. Veer away from the wall to descend to the valley floor and take the stone footbridge over a stream. Turn left immediately to go through a waymarked gate and walk with the stream on your left. Continue over a stile beside a gate at the end of this meadow. Pass woodland on your right to reach a waymarked gate in the next fence. Go ahead to reach a minor road.

Cross the road to take the signposted Windrush Way opposite, going ahead over a stile beside a gate. Follow the waymarked path which keeps to the higher ground to the south of the meandering River Windrush, which is on your left. Go over a succession of waymarked stiles then through a gate before veering right, as shown by a waymark post. A well-trodden path leads through gorse bushes.

Reach a broken wall and a fence ahead. Turn right, as waymarked, to put the fence on your left and continue through a waymarked gate to follow a track through a forest. A wall joins you on your left. Go ahead when it ends, ignoring crosspaths. Reach a waymark post near an old railway arch (on your right) and go ahead to climb above the trees on your left.

Bear right over a field to Aston Farm and continue to a lane. Turn left to take a bridge across the Windrush and pass houses. Reach a signposted bridleway junction and leave the Windrush Way by turning left along a hedged track. Continue past a field on your left and with a wall becoming a hedge on your right. Go through a gate to the next field and

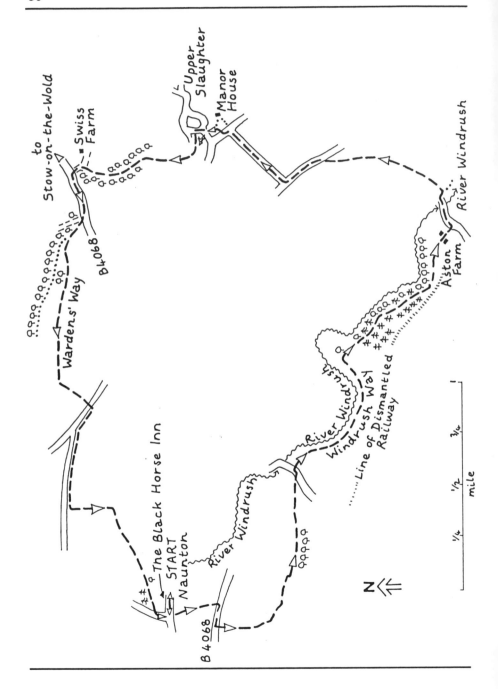

veer left with the track, but still keeping the hedge, becoming a wall, on your right. Continue along a walled path to a road.

Go left along the road until the first turning on your right. Turn right down this lane to Upper Slaughter. Turn left at the road junction overlooking the manor house. Look for a narrow, walled, path on your right and turn left when this emerges on a lane. Go right in the centre of the village and divert left to visit the church, if you wish.

Continue along the signposted Wardens' Way, soon passing a telephone box on your right. Turn left along a track signposted as a No Through Road, above the River Eye on your right. Continue through a waymarked gate to follow a fieldpath to a small wooden gate. Go ahead with a hedge on your right and pass Cress Cottage.

Go though a gate into woodland. Follow the muddy track with the river on your right. Pass a bridge giving access to Swiss Farm and reach the B4068 road. Go left for about 400 yards and pass a private drive (and public bridleway) on your right. Immediately after this, bear right along a rough lane. Notice a blue arrow with the Wardens' Way symbol on the first telegraph pole on your left, before a row of cottages.

Take the waymarked gate ahead to follow a stone wall on your left. Rise beside it to a waymarked gate in the top corner. Continue over a series of fields to a barn and yard. Leave through the waymarked gate and turn left down the track to a road.

Cross the road carefully and go through the small wooden gate ahead. Turn right, as signposted, to follow the bridleway (and Wardens' Way) parallel to the road on your right. When the wall on your right bends left, keep beside it and parallel to the lane that is now on its far side. Pass the access track to Brockhill Farm on your left.

Reach a roadside signpost and turn left along the track which here forms part of the Wardens' Way. Follow a wall on your left but ignore the track which bears left. Go ahead down the signposted bridleway, with a hedge now on your left. Bear right, as waymarked, in the bottom corner of the field. Cross a stream and follow a well-trodden path uphill. Cut across the corner of a field to a waymarked gap in the top wall. Continue through the waymarked gap in the far right corner ahead.

Descend to a belt of trees and follow the path down to a stile. This is beside a gate in the bottom corner of the next field. Reach a road and turn left along it into Naunton. Go left at the T-junction to return to the Black Horse Inn, on your left.

The Black Horse

8. BOURTON-ON-THE-WATER

Route: Bourton-on-the-Water – Wardens' Way – Lower Slaughter – Upper Slaughter – Oxfordshire Way – Bourton-on-the-Water

Distance: 6^1/$_2$ miles

Map: O.S. Pathfinder 1067 Winchcombe & Stow-on-the-Wold

Start: The Duke of Wellington Inn, Bourton-on-the-Water (Grid Reference: SP 167207)

Access: Bourton-on-the-Water was at the junction of the Fosse Way with Ryknild Street (from Alcester) in Roman times. It's now at the junction of the A429 and the A436. Unfortunately, it's no longer on the railway network. The Duke of Wellington Inn is in Sherborne Street, just off the High Street, and near the Cotswold Motor Museum and Village Life Exhibition. Cars can be parked around the corner in the High Street, or in a small car park for patrons at the rear of the pub. The Coach & Horses also has a car park. Buses stop in the High Street not far from the Duke of Wellington. They usually stop to set down or pick up passengers on request when passing the Coach & Horses. The chief bus service is run by Pulham's between Cheltenham and Moreton-in-Marsh, where there are railway stations. Telephone 0451 20369 for details.

The Duke of Wellington Inn (0451 20539

This 16th century village pub offers good food, comfortable accommodation and strong ales. Families are welcome to use the Garden room, while young adults have a special 'Trendy Duke' area kept separate for them. The riverside beer terrace would be an ideal place to relax in the evening after a day's ramble in the summer. Vegetarians are catered for. Opening hours are 11 a.m. to 3 p.m. and 6 p.m. to 1 p.m. on weekdays, 12 noon to 3 p.m. and 7 p.m. to 10.30 p.m. on Sundays.

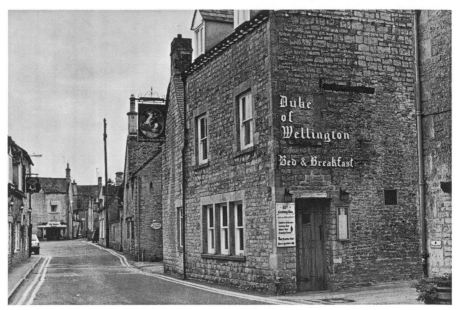

The Duke of Wellington

The Coach & Horses (0451 21064)

This friendly pub is passed on the outskirts of Bourton-on-the-Water, beside the Fosse Way. It's just the place the Romans might have built an inn, but this building dates from the 17th century. Real ales are served, including Flowers Original and Boddington's. There is a beer garden at the rear and meals are available. The opening hours are 11 a.m. to 2.30 p.m., and 7 p.m. to 11 p.m. from Monday to Friday; 11 a.m. to 3 p.m. and 7 p.m. to 11 p.m. on Saturday; 11 a.m. to 3 p.m. and 7 p.m. to 10.30 p.m. on Sunday.

Bourton-on-the-Water

'The Mini-Venice of the Cotswolds' is just one of this village's accolades. Even the sheer volume of the tourists cannot prevent the eye from admiring what has made Bourton-on-the-Water so popular. The sparkling waters of the River Windrush are crossed by a series of low, picturesque bridges. Running parallel to the attractive High Street, with its stone buildings, the river is bordered by trees and lawns. It comes as a surprise to learn that it was artificially channelled through the village in the 18th century, having previously meandered south of it.

People have lived on or very close to this site for at least 5000 years. A neolithic encampment near the estate at the end of this walk has also yielded Iron Age currency bars from about 300 BC. The Roman Second Legion of some 5000 soldiers was quartered here, building a bridge to carry the Fosse Way over the Windrush at Lansdown. There was a Saxon settlement here by 708, according to an old charter. It recorded a gift of land by King Cenred to Evesham Abbey in return for the building of a church at Bourton-on-the-Water and the provision of monks to spread the Gospel. Originally dedicated to St Mary the Virgin, the present parish Church of St Lawrence may go back to Roman times. There was certainly a pagan temple on its site.

The modern God is the tourist's money, with a host of 'attractions' catering for the visitors. Each is well worth a visit, even if the whole is to give the impression of a Blackpool in the Cotswolds. See, then, the Model Village (High Street, tel. 0451 20467) with its one-ninth scale replica complete with a model of the model.

The High Street also has a splendid Model Railway (tel. 0451 20686), while the Cotswold Motor Museum and Village Life Exhibition are housed in the Old Mill at the start of Sherborne Street (tel. 0451 21255). There is an Exhibition of Perfumery in Victoria Street (tel. 0451 20698) and a marvellous birdland, complete with flamingoes, penguins and parrots, in Rissington Road (tel. 0451 20689/20480).

You'll have no difficulty in buying postcards, fish and chips, candy floss, kiss-me-quick hats and so on.

Lower Slaughter

After the razzle-dazzle of Bourton, here is another attractive waterside location that is sedate and peaceful. The walk passes a well-preserved watermill at the Mill Bakery. The wheel survives, even if a brick chimney has been added for steam power to supplement the force of the river.

The Watermill, Lower Slaughter

Upper Slaughter

A tablet in St Peter's Church gives thanks for the safe return of all the village servicemen from both World Wars. This is one of the few 'thankful villages' not to need a war memorial.

The Oxfordshire Way

This extends for 65 miles to Henley-on-Thames, linking the Cotswolds with the Chilterns. Our route joins it at the site of the now-vanished Wyck Mill, beside the River Dikler.

The Walk

Go left from the Duke of Wellington to cross the bridge over the Windrush and pass the Motor Museum on your left. Turn left to pass the bus stop outside Windrush Newsagents (with parking spaces across the road on your right). Turn right along the metalled path to pass St Lawrence's Church on your right. Continue past school buildings on your left.

Turn left when you come to a road and follow the same pavement as the signposted Wardens' Way and the Heart of England Way. Pass a Roman Catholic chapel on your right. Go right along the path beside the A429 (Fosse Way) and approach the Coach & Horses. The route continues by turning left across the road (with care!).

Take the signposted Wardens' Way on the far side of the road. This is a metalled path all the way to Lower Slaughter, where you turn left on the signposted Wardens' Way. Walk with the River Eye on your left and parallel to the road on your right. Keep beside the river on your left to approach the old watermill.

Follow the road around the Mill Bakery and turn left with the signposted Wardens' Way. Continue through two kissing gates and past the long millpond on your left. Go ahead through a third kissing gate and veer slightly right across a field, as waymarked. Continue through a fieldgate and along the next field to a kissing gate.

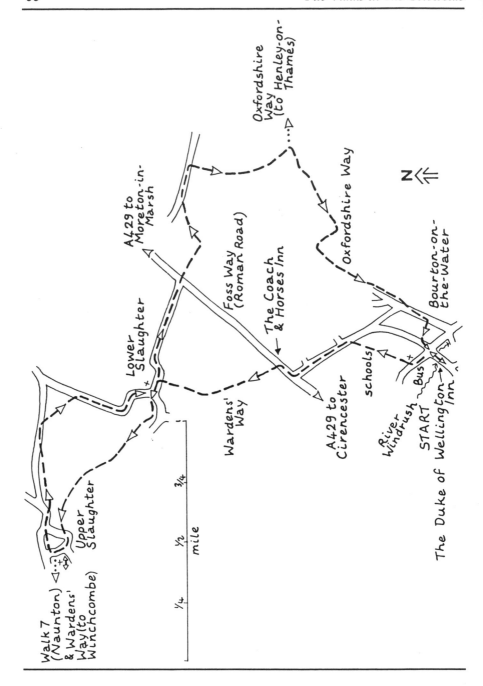

Go ahead between trees and descend to a waymarked kissing gate. Cross the footbridge after it to follow an enclosed path into Upper Slaughter. Turn left with the signposted Wardens' Way at a road, then take the path up to St Peter's Church on your right. Retrace your steps from the church and go left with the signposted Wardens' Way, soon passing a telephone box on your right.

Bear right with the road as it descends to a ford. Cross the River Eye by the accompanying footbridge and turn right over a waymarked stile to walk with the river on your right. Go left ahead when you reach a road. When the road bends left, go ahead through a gate on your right and turn left to walk parallel to the road.

Take a waymarked gate in the hedge ahead and keep parallel to the hedge of the road on your left. Continue through another waymarked gate and walk close to the hedge on your left until you can turn left over a stile in it, just before the corner of this field.

Turn right along the road for 200 yards, then bear right over a stile to follow a short path between trees to a second stile. Maintain your direction across the corner of a field and through a belt of trees to another road.

Go right to follow the road through Lower Slaughter, passing St Mary's Church on your left and continuing to the A429 (Fosse Way). Cross this road carefully to take the gate opposite and follow a signposted public bridleway. Go ahead through a second gate and turn left to follow the hedge for 75 yards before bearing right between fences.

Cross a bridge over a stream and go through a gate to reach a road. Go right to cross the old railway. Continue for 300 yards before turning right over a waymarked stile next to a gate. Ignore a track on your right but go ahead through the waymarked gate and walk beside a hedge on your left.

Continue through a gate ahead. Walk with a fence on your right to a waymarked gate in the hedge on your left. Go left through this and turn right immediately to walk with the hedge now on your right. Take the gate in the next corner. The right of way bears left across the next field, but you walk with the hedge on your right to a bridge over the River

Dikler. The right of way achieves this by making a 'dog leg' with a path that is part of the Oxfordshire Way.

Turn right over the bridge across the River Dikler to follow the waymarked Oxfordshire Way towards its western terminus at Bourton-on-the-Water. Continue over a second footbridge spanning the original course of the Dikler and a third footbridge crossing the River Eye. Walk with a hedge on your right to go over another footbridge and reach a kissing gate in the next corner.

Turn right along a muddy lane which soon bends left. Look for the Oxfordshire Way waymark and take a narrow, enclosed, path above the road on your right. Emerge on the pavement of Roman Way. Ignore a road on your right. Go ahead down Station Road to pass a garage on your right. Turn right along the signposted path just before Foxes Close on your right. Go right at a path junction to keep beside a wall on your left and reach Moore Road. Go left down to the High Street and cross it carefully to follow Sherborne Street back to the Duke of Wellington Inn on your right.

9. SEVEN SPRINGS

Route: Seven Springs – New Farm – Coberley – South Hill – Hartley Farm – Seven Springs

Distance: 6^1/$_2$ miles

Map: O.S. Pathfinder 1089 Gloucester

Start: The Seven Springs Inn (Grid Reference: SO967169)

Access: The Seven Springs Inn is on the A436 near its junction with the A435, about two miles south of Cheltenham. This junction is served on weekdays by bus no 151 between Cheltenham and Swindon via Cirencester.

The Seven Springs Inn (024287 219)

There wasn't a pub here until 1986, just a derelict 16th century barn. Now it has been tastefully converted and deserves your custom. Real ale is served, of course, while there is a restaurant which welcomes children and vegetarians. Opening hours are 11 a.m. to 2.30 p.m. and 6 p.m. to 11 p.m. on weekdays, 12 noon to 3 p.m. and 7 p.m. to 10.30 p.m. on Sundays.

Seven Springs

'Hic Tuus O Tamesine Pater Septemgeminus Fons' reads the inscription above these famous springs. Officialdom now prefers to recognise Thames Head, near Kemble, as the source of the River Thames. It is the River Churn that rises at Seven Springs, but this tributary of the Thames actually has its source further from the sea. The nearby Seven Springs House was built in the 1850s. Used by Cheltenham Ladies College during World War II, it housed a Girls' Preparatory School until the mid 1960s. It was converted to an Adventure School in 1978.

Coberley

Coberley was originally spelt Cubberley, derived from Cuthbert's ley. Ley is used here in the sense of a clearing. It is worth making the short diversion to visit the old church of St Giles. This is approached by a path going under an archway in a farm building. Its foundations are Norman, but it was rebuilt in the 19th century. The Berkeley family, who owned most of Gloucestershire in the 12th century, have many memorials here. Look in a recess in the sanctuary for the monument to Sir Giles Berkeley (died 1295). This is of a knight in chain-mail with his hands clasping a heart across a shield on his breast. Only the knight's heart is buried here – the rest of his body was buried at Little Malvern. The effigies of Sir Thomas Berkeley and his wife, Lady Joan, are on a large tomb in the south chapel. Sir Thomas died in 1352, six years after representing his country at the Battle of Crecy.

His widow survived him to marry Sir William Whittington and gave birth to the celebrated Dick Whittington, Lord Mayor of London. Dick was actually born at Pauntley Court, across the River Severn to the north-west of here, but he spent his childhood at Coberley Manor. This stood next to the church, with only the high walls of the churchyard and the large flat area beyond to show for it today.

If he did have to walk to London (he was the third son and the family was going through a bad patch), he soon made his fortune. He was recorded as lending money to the City, of London when he wasn't much older than 20. His prosperity was based on the cloth trade. When the Lord Mayor of London died in office in June 1397, the King (who also borrowed money from Whittington) appointed him as the successor.

His formal election by the Aldermen followed that October and he was re-elected in 1406 and 1419. He died in 1423, when he must have been in his sixties. Apart from lending money to both Henry IV and Henry V, he administered the expenses for the completion of Westminster Abbey.

Sadly, he was a widower without any children. His vast fortune was left to charity, paying for the modernisation of Newgate Prison, the founding of a hospital and a library, the installation of a public water tap in Cripplegate and, it is believed, the repair of Gloucester Cathedral. By 1605 his fame had been commemorated in a popular ballad about Dick

Whittington and his cat. The manor house, where Charles I stayed during the Civil War, was demolished in 1790. It fell into disrepair after its owner was ruined in the South Sea Bubble financial collapse of 1720.

The Walk

First, make your pilgrimage to the Seven Springs. Cross the road from the inn to the lay-by on your left. The Seven Springs are down steps between the lay-by and the A436. Return to this road and go left, passing the inn on your right, to its crossroads with the A435. Cross this carefully to take the path opposite, signposted 'To the Cotswold Way Alternative Route'.

Seven Springs

Go through, a wooden gate and along the farm track ahead, with a fence on your left and a hedge on your right. Bear right as you climb to pass a copse on your left. Continue along the track to a lane, where you go left for 300 yards. Then, turn sharply right up a private road – actually, a rough track that is also a public path.

Pass a bungalow on your left and a barn on your right. Take a grassy track ahead,

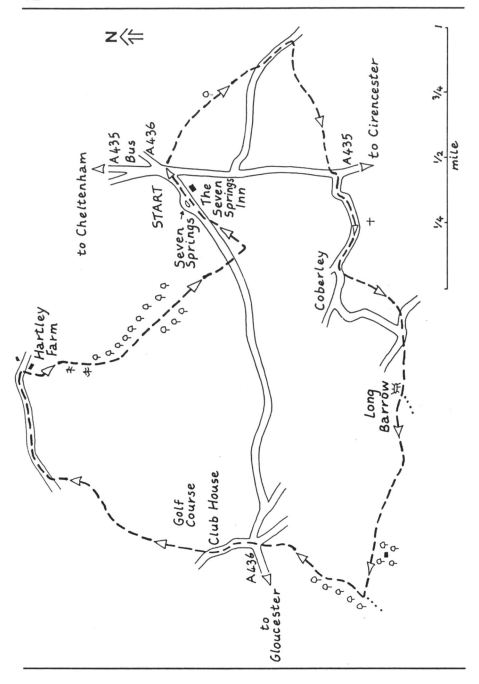

keeping beside the hedge on your left. Descend with this to a path which leaves the bottom-left corner of the next field and emerges at the A435. Turn left for 50 yards, then take the road for Coberley, on your right.

Pass farm buildings and the church behind them on your left. Fork left as you enter the village of Coberley, passing the Post Office on your right. Immediately afterwards, turn left through a low wooden gate and down a signposted and waymarked path, walking with a hedge on your left. Cross a small footbridge and a stile.

Go ahead over a second stile and follow a wooden fence (on your right) to a stile beside a gate in the next corner. Continue past a farm on your right along a track. Go with a wall on your right at a junction, take the gate ahead and keep beside the wall on your right as you follow a road.

Ignore a road to your right at a junction, but go straight ahead up a signposted path. Reach an ancient barrow on your right and bear right with the main path, ignoring another going through a gate on your left. Climb gradually and veering right to a stile beside a gate in the wall ahead. Continue to pass a farm sheltered by trees on your left and reach a signpost at a T-junction before the wood ahead.

Turn right down a track to the A436. Cross it carefully and go up the lane opposite. Pass a Golf Club House on your right, then turn right along the signposted Cotswold Way towards Leckhampton Hill. The fenced track passes the golf course on your right and leads to a minor road. Go right along this.

Just before Hartley farm, turn right along the signposted path back to Coberley. Begin with the wall on your left. Turn left over a waymarked stile and bear right to follow the path in the bottom of the valley. Pass a plantation of conifers on your right. Cross a stile beside a gate ahead to walk beside a wall and a fence on your left.

Pass under power lines and turn left over a stile beside a gate. Step into the neck of a long field. Walk with the fence on your left at first, then switch to follow the opposite fence, with trees behind it. Go ahead over a waymarked stile in the far corner of this field.

Continue with a hedge on your left and cross a stile at the bottom of the next field to reach the A436 again. Go left for 20 yards, then cross the road carefully to take the path which descends beside the hedge running ahead on your left. Turn left over a waymarked stile in the next corner and follow the narrow, fenced, path back to the road. Turn right for the Seven Springs Inn.

The Seven Springs Inn

10. PAINSWICK HILL AND STREAM

Route: The Royal William Inn – Painswick Hill – Painswick – Damsells Mill – The Royal William Inn

Distance: $5^1/_2$ miles

Maps: O.S. Pathfinders 1089 Gloucester and 1113 Stroud

Start: The Royal William Inn (Grid Reference: SO879127)

Access: The Royal William Inn is on the western side of the A46 – about two miles north of Painswick and just south of Gloucester and Cheltenham. There is a car park and a bus stop for the no. 46 service between Stroud and Cheltenham (weekdays only).

The Royal William Inn (0452 813650)

William IV was the king who preceded Queen Victoria and reigned from 1830 to 1837. This pub commemorates both his accession to the throne and the opening of what was then the new turnpike road to Cheltenham. It is now a popular place for meals and bar snacks. Real ale (including Pompey Royal) is served and the opening hours are 11 a.m. to 11 p.m. daily.

Painswick Beacon

The Cotswold Way is followed past the beech trees of Pope's Wood (a nature reserve with a name inspired by Prinknash Abbey at its foot) to one of the most invigorating and stimulating places along the whole of the Cotswold escarpment. Painswick Beacon stands at 913 feet above sea level, in 250 acres of common land. It can become very busy with walkers and golfers at weekends. The Forest of Dean can be seen across the Severn to the west, while the Malverns are easy to identify to the north. This spectacular site contains Kimsbury Camp, an Iron Age hillfort. Triangular in shape, this has double ramparts and ditches plus a very steep slope to the north. The main entrance has been identified in the south-east but the interior has been ruined by quarrying. Charles I's demoralised army had to suffer a night of 'tempestuous rainy weather' exposed here.

Painswick

Wool and the pure Cotswold water brought prosperity to this town, especially in the 18th century. This is where the cloth was dyed. The handsome buildings, such as the early Georgian Dover House, testify to the expertise of the local stonemasons, and to the durability of the local Jurassic limestone. Masons were also kept busy making table tombs in the 18th century. Buy pamphlets in the church to two 'tomb trails'. Ninety-nine yew trees were planted in 1792. It is a contest to count these accurately (some are intertwined) to confirm or refute the tale that the devil won't let the one hundredth tree survive.

Painswick has retained its reputation for craftwork and there is no better example of this than the embroidered kneelers in St Mary's church. This colourful and interesting collecting represents the life and work of the people of Painswick, including the Ramblers. The church has a 17th century spire on top of its 15th century tower, but this may have been a holy spot for thousands of years. Feast Sunday in mid-September may be a folk memory of pagan times. Robert Raikes, the founder of Sunday Schools, considered that it 'would have disgraced a heathen nation'. Known as the Clipping Service and held in the open air, children now hold hands (clipping means embracing and has nothing to do with the 99 yew trees) and dance around the church. Flowers are worn in the hair and 'Painswick Buns' are consumed.

Just to give an idea of the time scale here, New Street dates back to 1492 and replaced Bisley Street, which dates from 1260, as the main thoroughfare. As you approach Painswick, don't miss the Rococo Gardens of Painswick House. These are open from February to mid-December, Wednesday to Saturday plus Bank Holiday Mondays, between 11 a.m. and 5 p.m. They have been restored to their original form as depicted in an 18th century painting.

Damsells Mill

Highgrove House is passed on the way to this, but it's not the home of the Waleses (see the walk south of Tetbury for that). Damsells Mill, which earns its name from its constant chattering noise, dates from the 17th century and has been both a cloth and a corn mill. Walking ahead beside Painswick Stream, pass Tocknells Court. This grand house dates from 1665 and has colourful formal gardens.

The Walk

Facing the Royal William Inn, go right and immediately left to follow the access drive which goes behind the inn. The beech trees of Buckholt Wood are on your right, from where the signposted Cotswold Way comes to join the lane. Pass Castle Lodge on your left and the nature reserve of Pope's Wood on your right. Fork right up a rough track signposted as the Cotswold Way, passing a golf course on your left and woodland on your right.

The Royal William

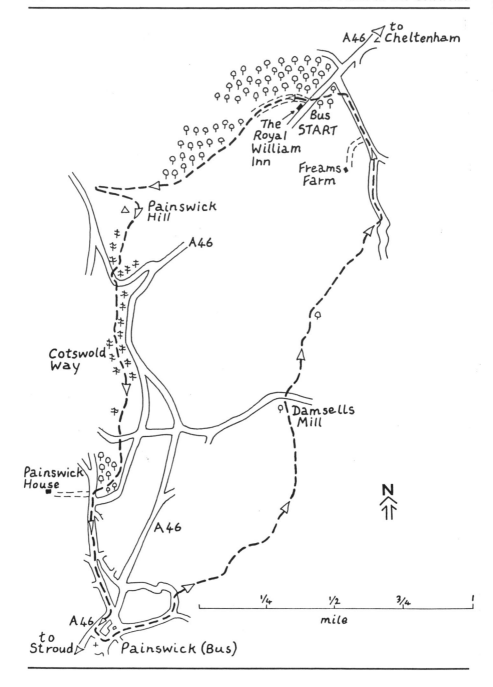

You can wander over the common straight to Painswick Beacon, ahead. But this route veers right along the right of way, beside the perimeter fence of the wood on your right. Ignore tracks joining from the right as you descend, but turn sharply left before the road ahead. Follow the grassy track back up the golf course to the summit of Painswick Hill.

Go right and descend along a path past pine trees on your right. Reach a road and go left, with the signposted Cotswold Way. When the road bends left, bear right, again along the signposted Cotswold Way. Pass the redundant Catsbrain Quarry on your right, following the narrow path waymarked with yellow arrows plus the white dot of the Cotswold Way.

Gradually descend through trees. Emerge from them to fork right along the waymarked Cotswold Way. Cross part of the golf course to pass the cemetery on your left. Continue over a road at a waymark post and descend to the bottom corner ahead. Follow a path through the trees on your right to the B4073 (main road to Gloucester). The entrance to Painswick House and its Rococo Gardens is opposite.

Turn left along the road down to Painswick. Go right at a fork along Gloucester Road and turn right at New Street to reach St Mary's church. From its porch, bear left to leave the churchyard and pass the house (on your left) where the composer Charlie Wilfred Orr (born 1893) lived from 1934 to his death in 1976. There is a plaque outside.

Go up St Mary's Street, pass the Royal Oak Inn on your right and continue down Vicarage Street. Notice Dover House's fine Georgian masonry on your right. Keep left when a road descends towards Sheepscombe on your right. Pass Verlands on your right, followed by Tithe Cottage, and bear right along a signposted lane. Go ahead 100 yards to a stile on your right.

Bear right over the wooden stile to walk down a field to another stile. Cross this and a bridged stream to bear right, as waymarked. Go over a stone stile above a gate in the far corner. Join a lane and take the small gate beside a fieldgate across it before a cattle grid. Pass Highgrove House on your left and continue over a stile beside a gate. Pass a ruined circular building on your right. Cross two stiles beside a gate ahead on your left. Walk with a hedge on your right in the next field. Cross a bridge over a stream to a waymarked path junction.

Turn left and keep close to Painswick Stream in what becomes almost a ravine on your left. Reach a road at Damsells Mill (on your left and now a private house). Follow the yellow waymarked path straight ahead, crossing a stile beside a gate to keep the stream on your left. Cross two more stiles beside gates in a series of meadows, then veer left towards the stream.

Stile near Damsells Mill

Go over a stile to enter a spinney at the site of Oliver's Mill. The ruins include a dam and sluices but are not on the right of way. Take the stepping stones across the stream on your left and bear right to pass a cottage on your left.

Go ahead over a stile beside a gate and up a long pasture in which you keep the stream on your right. Cross a stile beside the gate in the far right corner. Do not go ahead across the bridge! Go left to pass Tocknells Court on your left and follow its access drive with the stream on your right.

Turn left up a road and pass the access track to Freams Farm on your left. Continue with a hedge on your left until it ends and bear left along a woodland path. Emerge at the A46 and go left to cross it carefully to the Royal William Inn.

11. ELKSTONE

Route: The Green Dragon Inn – Cockleford – Elkstone – Gloucester Beeches – The Golden Heart Inn – Cowley Wood – The Green Dragon Inn.

Distance: 6 miles

Map: O.S. Pathfinder 1089 Gloucester

Start: The Green Dragon Inn, Cockleford (Grid Reference: S0969142)

Access: Take the A435 in a southerly direction from Cheltenham towards Cirencester. After about five miles, you will see a signpost to Elkstone. Turn right, follow the road around a sweeping bend and you will find the Green Dragon Inn on your left. There is an ample car park, while the nearest bus stop is less than a quarter of a mile away where the road for Elkstone leaves the A435. This is for the X51 service between Cheltenham and Swindon via Cirencester. Latest timetable information is available from Gloucestershire County Council (tel: 0452 425543). Currently, there are five buses in each direction every weekday (no Sunday service).

The Green Dragon Inn (0242 – 870271 or 870523)

Originally called the Cockleford Arms, its name seems to have been acquired fairly recently, but there's plenty of fire in this dragon. Come on a Monday night for live jazz, or make it a Wednesday evening for live folk music. The main building began as a house, while the barn overlooking Cowley Lake to the left used to be the local farriers. Its position on the old road between Gloucester and Oxford led to cider being sold from it in the 17th century and a pub being established. A huge selection of Real Ale is available, as is food, including several choices of vegetarian dishes. Children are welcome both in the Top Room off one bar and in the Sunday Carvery. The bar staff have been known to ramble the local paths in their free time. Opening hours are 11 a.m. to 2.30 p.m. and 6 p.m. to 11 p.m. on weekdays, with a 12 noon start on Sundays.

The Golden Heart Inn (0242-87261)

At the risk of distracting drinkers from the serious business of walking (with two of the six miles still to go), the Golden Heart Inn has catered for wayfarers since at least the early 16th century. There is even archaeological evidence for a Roman drinking-place here, in the days when the legions tramped along Ermin Way, now the A417 between Gloucester and Cirencester. There is a good selection of food and real ales. Children are welcome and there is bed and breakfast accommodation. Opening hours are 10.30 a.m. to 3 p.m. and 6 p.m. to 11 p.m.

The Golden Heart Inn

Elkstone

Ley hunters will know to expect an ancient standing stone at a place name incorporating the word 'stone'. Head for St John's church to find the favourite candidate for 'Ealac's stone'. This is the smaller one attached to the back wall of the vestry. Notice its carving, which may be of Saxon origin. The Saxons adopted, or recognised, ancient stones as definite boundary markers.

The original purpose of the stones may have been more sacred. Smaller stones, or even one big stone which is now broken into pieces, may have stood in the churchyard. There is a line of stones, or fragments of a stone, beside the path near the entrance gate. The footpath from the village to the church is the old coffin path.

The church dates from about 1160 and is famous for a carved tympanum on the shouldered arch over the south door. Our Lord, on a cushioned throne, holds the Book of Judgement in his left hand, while giving the Blessing with his right. The symbols of the four evangelists are below, with the Agnus Dei above on the left. The hand of God is in the panel above Jesus.

Elkstone Church

Go round to the west door to see a curious symbol – an Egyptian *ankh* (symbol of eternal life). The building in the south-eastern corner of the churchyard is the priest's house, dating from the 14th century. Inside, look at the rare instance of 12th century zig-zag carving at the east end of the chancel. The 15th century font has exceptionally good craftsmanship. A second, larger stone, at the back of the vestry is a grave cover with a wheel-cross and dates from the 13th century.

The tower was erected in the 15th century to replace a central tower which fell down in the 13th century. Not far from this windswept village is the Roman road known as Ermin Way. This route began in Silchester, went through Cirencester and followed the high ground before descending to Gloucester. It is not straight, having to alter course to keep to the highest ground. The layby at Gloucester Beeches is on the ancient road as the A417 has been realigned at this point. The original Roman destination, via a zig-zag descent at Birdlip, was a fort at Kingsholm. This is now a suburb to the north of Gloucester. Glevum, as the Romans called the city, was built when this site suffered from flooding. The A417 now follows the Roman route almost exactly between Cirencester and Birdlip.

The Walk

With your back to The Green Dragon Inn, go left and uphill. Ignore a signposted stile on your right (you will return over it). Turn left to follow a No Through Road towards Cockleford. Pass a path signposted on your left and go round a bend on your right.

Turn right off the road just before a signpost. Take the first of two metal fieldgates, with a waymark on the post between them. Veer right to a footbridge and use it to cross a brook. Go left past conifer trees on your right and follow the path through more scrubby woodland ahead. Go through a small waymarked wooden gate and turn left to follow the waymarked route past a wood on your left and around boggy patches. Reach a small wooden gate giving access to a road.

Turn right along the road for 10 yards, then turn left over a stone stile to follow a signposted path across a field. This gradually converges with the hedge on your right. Go ahead over a stone stile to pass a house on your right. Turn right, as waymarked, to cross a stile at the end of the wall ahead. A metalled drive leads you left into the village of Elkstone.

Go right at the road for 10 yards, then turn left along a rough private road which is signposted as a public path. This soon bends right to reach

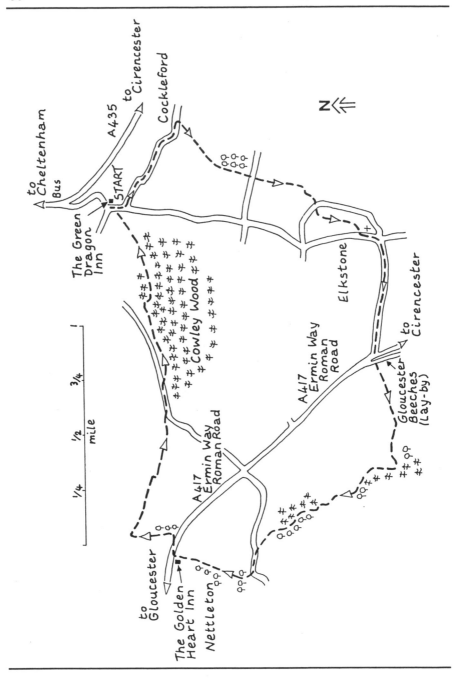

the metal gate of The Vernals. Turn left just before it, along an enclosed path. Go ahead over a stile into a paddock. Leave by a stile in the opposite fence and continue past a wall on your left to a stone stile in the wall ahead.

Veer very slightly right (keeping beside a fence on your left) to the church of St John the Evangelist. Continue along the road, passing the church on your left and soon reaching a crossroads. Turn right along a road. Ignore the signposted path forking left from it. Go ahead across the A417 and the layby which marks the actual line of the Roman Ermin Way.

Ahead of you are two signposted rights of way. Take the bridleway on your right, crossing the wooden stile to the right of a metal fieldgate. Walk along the edge of a field on your right, keeping near a wall on your left. Go ahead through two more fieldgates, then veer right as the wall bears left. Descend towards a forest.

Turn right along a track to pass the forest on your left. Ignore a track into the forest. Go ahead through a wooden gate waymarked with a blue arrow. Pass a lake (with a swan) on your right.

Fork right to take the lower track and soon turn right, as waymarked by yellow arrows, down to a wooden footbridge. Cross both it, a subsequent footbridge and a stile. Veer left, as waymarked. Cross a stile in the corner of the field and continue to join a rough track to a wooden gate.

Continue as waymarked, ignoring a gate into a conifer plantation on your right, but crossing a stile into woodland soon after it. Go ahead through the trees and with a stream on your right. Yellow arrows painted on trees lead you to wooden steps up to a wooden gate below a house on your left.

Follow the right of way as marked by arrows. It drops below the access lane only to rejoin it and reach a road at a signpost. Go left for 250 yards then turn right over a stile. Follow the signposted path as it descends with a fence on your right.

Turn right over a stile and turn left immediately to descend through trees. Go right to pass a gate on your left and walk with a hedge (changing to a wall) on your left. Maintain this direction uphill, passing a second gate and walking with a fence on your left. Take a gate ahead. Eventually go through a waymarked gate to pass The Golden Heart Inn on your left.

Cross the A417 (Ermin Way) with great care. Go right to find a path veering left after 50 yards. Turn left over a stile beside a gate and follow the signposted path. Reach a stile in a distant top fence. Cross it and go right along a rough track.

Continue along a bridleway at a signposted junction. When the farm track turns left with a wall, turn right, as waymarked, for 25 yards. Turn left to follow another wall on your left. Fork left in the bottom corner of a field to follow the path waymarked with yellow arrows. Go over stiles to reach a road on your right.

Go left down the road (ignoring an uphill lane facing you). Ignore a signposted footpath on your right, but fork right along a bridleway at a second roadside signpost. Take a small metal gate to walk along the edge of a long field on your left and beside a wood on your right.

Go ahead through a gate into the wood, bear right with the track to a junction. Turn left to follow the route waymarked with blue arrows and pass conifer trees on your right. Emerge through a gate to follow a fence on your left to a road. From here, turn left to return to The Green Dragon Inn.

12. COLESBOURNE & WITHINGTON WOODS

Route: Colesbourne – Cott Plantation – Chedworth – Withington Woods – Coiesbourne

Distance: 10 miles

Maps: O.S. Pathfinders 1089 Gloucester and 1090 Northleach & Andoversford

Start: The Colesbourne Inn (Grid Reference: SO999133)

Access: The Colesbourne Inn is on the A435 about six miles south of Cheltenham. There is a bus stop nearby for the weekday service no X51 between Cheltenham and Swindon via Cirencester.

The Colesbourne Inn (024287 376)

Travellers along the then new main road between Cheltenham and Cirencester have found hospitality at this inn since the reign of George III, over two hundred years ago. Recently, the old stable block has been converted into bedrooms. If you stay overnight here, however, you may be woken up by the ghost of Jack the Stable Lad, who committed suicide here over a century ago. He appears to favour the Nettlestone bedroom, which is notoriously cold. There is a large car park for patrons, a beer garden and Wadworth Ales from the wood. Bar snacks are available, or you could dine in the Brambles Restaurant. Opening hours are 11 a.m. to 3 p.m. and 6 p.m. to 11 p.m. on weekdays, 12 noon to 3 p.m. and 7 p.m. to 10.30 p.m. on Sundays.

Colesbourne

This is an ancient site beside the River Churn. An Iron Age coin inscribed with the name of the chieftain of the Dobunni tribe, Bodvoc, who came to terms with the invading Romans, has been found in the parish. The earliest record of the place-name is in the time of Coenwulf, King of Mercia in the late eighth century. Places which have 'cole' in their names are usually very old. Alfred Watkins, of 'The Old Straight Track' fame, found that where cole was an element, in a place-name, there was a ley. 'Cole' stems from 'coel', the Welsh word for an omen. The 'coleman' gave his name to places on the leys. He may have been a wizard who divined their courses, in company with the 'dodman' (a surveyor) and the 'blake or blackman' (who lit the beacons).

Perhaps it is this image of the 'coleman' which inspired the nursery rhyme about Old King Cole. Legend does account for a specific King Coel, however. He was a native ruler of Britain when this island was a client kingdom within the Roman Empire. Coel was the son of Lucius (himself a son of an earlier Coel and the great-grandson of Caractacus). He helped to establish Christianity as the state religion of Britain in the second half of the second century, thereby founding the first Christian nation. Coel reigned from Colchester (but did not give his name to the place). His daughter, Helena, married Constantius Chlorus and gave birth to Constantine, later known as the Great. As emperor of Rome, Constantine espoused the cause of Christianity, while his mother went to Jerusalem to discover the true cross. His grandfather, King Coel, is reputedly buried at Glastonbury.

There is more than one version of the original Old King Cole, however. One of the earliest examples of the nursery rhyme was collected by Robert Burns, in Ayrshire at the end of the 18th century. The first stanza runs as follows:

> Four auld King Coul was a jolly auld soul
> And a jolly auld soul was he
> Our auld King Coul fill'd a jolly brown bowl
> And he ca'd for his fiddlers three
> Fidell didell, fidell didell quo'the fiddlers
> There's no a lass in a'Scotland
> Like our sweet Marjorie.

This may be a folk memory of Coilus, an early fifth century King of the Britons in the region north of Hadrian's War. The Britons had allied with the Romans to repel the Scots and Picts, while maintaining their sense of sturdy independence. When the legions left, they provided military leadership for the British, with Cunedda moving down to North Wales where he drove out the Irish. Coilus attempted to play off the Scots against the Picts. A British kingdom survived in Strathclyde until its peaceful absorption into Scotland in 1018. The persistence of what became known as the Welsh language in Strathclyde and Cumbria until the 14th century is a testament to his reputation as Old Coel the Splendid *(Coel Hen Guotepauc).*

St James' Church, Colesbourne, contains a late 13th century pointed chancel arch. The manor house used to stand beside the church. John Elwes engaged the architect David Brandon to build something much bigger in 1851 and sailed off around the Mediterranean in his schooner while it was being built. He returned in 1854 to a bill of £19,384.

St James Church, Colesbourne

This house was taken over by the Ministry of Aircraft Production as drawing offices in World War II, with work being done on the Gloster Meteor jet. Never fully reoccupied, it was demolished in 1958, except one room which was incorporated into a new house which was rebuilt on the same site. The surrounding parkland contains over 200 different types of tree, collected by the traveller and naturalist Henry Elwes (1846-1922). Altogether, he planted about 600 acres of new woodland. Henry Elwes also worked with Lord Winchelsea and Shepherd Hall of Colesbourne to create a National Agricultural Union for landowners, tenant farmers and labourers. Lord Winchelsea's failing health prevented its establishment. Three separate bodies were eventually formed – the Country Landowners' Association, the National Farmers Union and the National Union of Agricultural and Allied Workers. Colesborne was also progressive in the field of parish councils. It formed the country's first on an experimental basis in 1892, only to have it taken away by the Local Government Act of 1894 because the village had less than 300 inhabitants!

The Walk

With your back to The Colesbourne Inn, go left along the pavement of the A435, towards Cirencester. Divert left, as signposted, to visit St James' Church, then resume your former direction, passing a garage on your left.

Turn left down the road signposted 'Withington 2^1/$_2$'. Follow this across the River Churn and climb to a corner where the road bends left. Go straight ahead along a track through the edge of a wood, Cott Plantation, on your left.

Continue along the track past a field on your left and with a hedge on your right. The track goes into forestry at the end of the field, bearing left. Well before this, however, there is a possibly-obscured and muddy track which forks right. Go down this to emerge at the corner of two fields.

Go ahead through the metal fieldgate and bear right along a grassy track to reach a wooden gate. Pass through this and take the sunken path which has a fence above it on your right. Go through a gate in the corner and follow the perimeter fence of a conifer plantation on your left.

Continue along the field's right-hand edge to a gate in the next corner. Go through this and walk beside a wall on your left. Reach a signposted junction and take a farm access lane ahead. This leads to a crossroads, where you cut across a central triangle of grass to bear right along the road signposted for Chedworth.

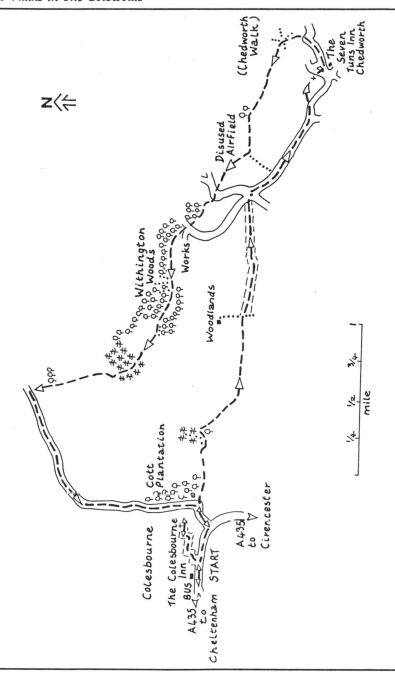

N

(Chedworth Walk)

The Seven Tuns Inn Chedworth

Disused Airfield

Withington Woods

Works

Woodlands

Cott Plantation

Colesbourne

The Colesbourne Inn

A435 BUS to Cheltenham   START

A435 to Cirencester

¼   ½   ¾   mile

Go left when this road forks. Turn left over a signposted stone stile at Manor Farm, where the road bends right. Follow the grassy path between an avenue of trees and parallel to a drive on your left. Take a stone stile in the corner ahead and bear right down to St Andrew's Church, Chedworth.

Bear right down to, the Seven Tuns Inn, Chedworth, where this route links with that to Chedworth Roman Villa. Turn left to pass the pub on your right and walk through the village. Climb to a corner where the road bends right and a private drive to Hartshill goes left. Go ahead through a hunting gate along a signposted path. Climb with a Fence, then a wall, on your left. Go through a small metal gate ahead to join a track coming from your right at a sharp angle. Go ahead through a metal fieldgate to a path junction.

Ignore a waymarked stile on your left, but bear left along the next path on your left. Walk beside a wall on your left and a fence on your right. Continue through a small, wooden, gate. Ignore a similar gate on your left immediately after it and go ahead with the line of a broken wall on your left and a field on your right.

Take the left-hand of two gates ahead. Continue in the next field with a broken wall on your right and a field on your left. Take a gate in the corner and walk with a wall on your right. The gate in the following corner leads to a copse.

Walk past the trees of the copse on your right, then with a wall and a hedge on your right. Look for a gap ahead and go through it. Reach an old airfield perimeter road. Go left along this until it bends left. At this point, bear half-right across what is now a cultivated field to a waymark post at the cross formed by two runways in the centre of the airfield. Don't turn sharply left down the long runway. Bear left along the shorter side-runway to reach a stile beside a signpost on its right-hand side where a fence crosses it.

Go ahead across a road and rejoin the old runway on the far side. Turn right just before a metal gate ahead and follow a narrow, waymarked, path. Enter woodland and turn left along a path which runs between a wall on your left and trees on your right. Gross a stile to go the other side of the wall and continue to a road.

Turn right for a few paces, then turn left to cross the road carefully and take the lane opposite you. This bears left to a works, while you go ahead through a small gate beside a larger one to follow a track. This passes Withington Woods on your right.

Pass a house on your left and keep to the broad track ahead, ignoring turnings, especially into the wood on your right. Bear right with the broad track to take a gate out of the wood and follow a hedge on your left past a field on your right.

The clear track continues through a gate in the corner of the field and leads past more trees and fields to a road. Turn left down this, bending left with it to rejoin your outward route near the River Churn. Follow this road back to the A435 and turn right back to The Colesbourne Inn.

The Colesbourne Inn

13. CHEDWORTH ROMAN VILLA

Route: Chedworth – Roman Villa – Yanworth Mill – Stowell Mill – Chedworth

Distance: $6^1/_2$ miles

Map: O.S. Pathfinder 1090 Northleach & Andoversford

Start: The Seven Tuns Inn, Chedworth (Grid Reference: SP052120)

Access: The Seven Tuns Inn is in the centre of Chedworth below the church. The infrequent local bus services are designed to give villagers a weekly shopping trip to Cirencester. But, they don't allow an outsider time to enjoy a walk from Chedworth in between buses. If you rely on public transport, combine this route with that from Colesbourne. Allow for a long day of 16 miles, plus a visit to Chedworth Roman Villa. There are pubs at both Colesbourne and Chedworth, however, while the bus service to Colesbourne is good from Mondays to Saturdays (no Sunday service). There is a bus (no. X51) between Cheltenham and Swindon via Cirencester.

The Seven Tuns Inn (0285 720242)

Ramblers are requested to use the public bar in this establishment, which doesn't welcome muddy boots! Perhaps the management hasn't recovered from the Civil War, when Cromwell billeted his troops here. A drinking-house has existed on this site since at least 1610. Real ale and food are available. Opening hours are 12 noon to 3 p.m. and 6 p.m. to 11 p.m. on weekdays; 12 noon to 3 p.m. and 7 p.m. to 10.30 p.m. on Sundays.

Seven Tuns Inn

Chedworth

Oh, for the days when you could reach this beautiful spot by train on the old Midland and South Western Junction Railway! This was opened in 1891 as a link across Great Western Railway territory between the London and South Western Railway at Andover and the Midland Railway at Cheltenham. As a main line to Southampton from the industrial North and Midlands, it came into its own during the build-up to D-Day in 1944. Closure came on 9th September 1961, although two pages of services were accidentally included in the timetable for 1961/62.

Now, even the railway viaduct that used to cross the village street has gone. A section of the dismantled line can be walked in the delightful woodland at the back of Chedworth Roman Villa.

First, however, visit St Andrew's Church, near the Seven Tuns Inn. This is a fine old Norman church, rebuilt in 1461 with the proceeds of the wool trade. Elizabeth of York, wife of King Henry VII, visited the completed church and now has her head carved in a corner of the nave.

A male head in the south-west corner is that of her husband, the first of the Tudor dynasty, while St Andrew is in the north-east corner. The two heads over the porch are probably of Anne Neville, whose family had been Lords of the Manor of Chedworth for 400 years, and her husband, the 'Kingmaker' and Duke of Warwick.

Chedworth Roman Villa

The Romans obviously knew how to choose a good site for a villa. Delightful beech and oak woodlands clothe the slopes on three sides of its remains, while the view from the fourth is over the peaceful valley of the River Coln. This is the finest of more than a dozen villas found within a ten-mile radius of Cirencester. It was only found by accident 1n 1864 when Eldon's gamekeeper was digging to retrieve a lost ferret. He unearthed a mosaic pavement. Extensive excavation has since shown that the villa began as separate buildings in the first half of the second century AD. A fire early in the third century led to rebuilding and enlargement.

The Roman Villa

All the buildings were connected by a continuous corridor in the fourth century. This created an inner courtyard, probably containing a private garden. A furnace room beyond the kitchen provided heat for a large dining room, whose mosaic floor depicted the four seasons. Two sets of baths, old and new, have been discovered. The site was supplied with water by a spring, which was covered by a small building known as the Nymphaeum. This was originally dedicated to a water goddess, but chi-rho symbols on the stone surround of the reservoir suggest Christianisation. A new dining room and guest suite with hypocaust were added in the late fourth century, not long before Britain was required by Rome to look to its own defence. Now in the care of the National Trust, a nine minute video programme can be seen in the museum. It is open from March to October from 10 a.m. to 5.30 p.m. daily, except on Mondays. It is, however, open on Bank Holiday Mondays (but closed on Good Friday).

The Walk

With your back to the Seven Tuns Inn, go right along the road through the village. This climbs to a corner where the road bends right and a private drive to Hartshill goes left. Go ahead through a small wooden gate along a signposted path. Climb with a fence, then a wall, on your left. Go ahead through a small metal gate to join a track coming sharply from your right. Take the metal fieldgate ahead to a path junction.

Ignore the path over a waymarked stile on your left. Ignore, too, the waymarked path, going half-left with a wall on your left and a fence on your right (this is the return route of the Colesbourne walk). You go straight ahead along a path between a fence on your left ant a wall on your right. There is another path to be ignored at this junction – going to your right between a fence and a hedge. Descend through woodland and bear right to pass a footpath signpost. Fork left to walk with a fence on your right and trees on your left.

Go ahead through a wooden gate waymarked with a blue arrow to reach a road. Go left to the Roman villa. Return down the road from the Roman villa and pass the path you came along out of the wood on your right. Continue to a crossroads, where you turn right through a wooden gate and follow a private road which is also a public footpath. This soon

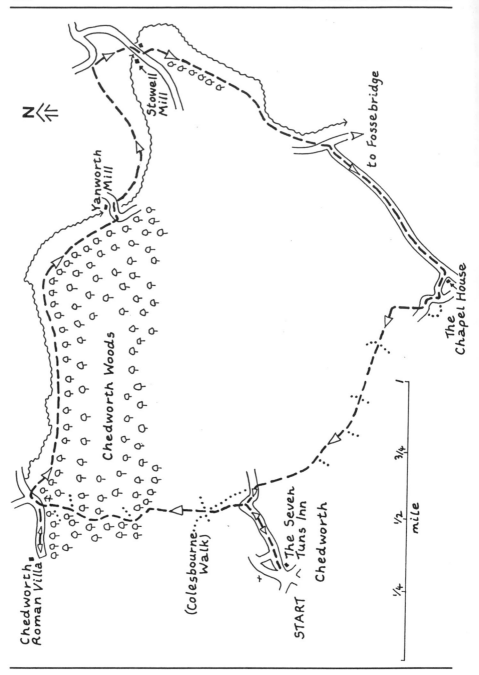

becomes a rough track, between the River Coln on your left and Chedworth Woods on your right.

Reach a road at its corner and turn left along it to cross the River Coln. Turn right opposite Yanworth Mill to take a path through a small wooden gate, waymarked with a yellow arrow. Walk beside a wall and a hedge on your right. Continue along this path until you reach another road.

Turn right immediately after gaining the road and take the waymarked path through a gate. Cross a field to a stone stile just to the left of Stowell Mill. Turn right along the road to pass the mill and a house opposite it, then turn left when there is a gap in the wall on your left. Go ahead through a small wooden gate next to a fieldgate to enter a meadow.

Turn right along a grassy track which passes a wood on your right. Maintain this direction past a hedge on your right and the River Coln on your left. Cross a stone stile in a wall ahead and veer right over the next field to take a small wooden gate onto a road. Turn left for 50 yards, then turn right up the road signposted for Chedworth.

Go right when the road forks, opposite a footpath signpost on your left. Pass the Chapel House on your left. Turn right with the road towards Greenhill Farm. Follow the road as it bends left, then right. Reach a signpost and go ahead up a rough track signposted as a public path and ignore the signposted footpath on your left along Greenhill Farm's private road. Walk with a wall on your left and trees or your right.

Turn left at the top of the hill to follow the fenced track. This is like a ridgeway path above the village of Chedworth on your left. Keep to it, going ahead with the blue arrow at the first crosspaths. Ignore later stiles to left and right, and a track descending on your left. Continue to a road and turn left down it back to Chedworth's Seven Tuns Inn. Should you be combining this walk with the Colesbourne route, pick up the returning path on your right when the road makes a sharp bend. This is where this route sets out from Chedworth.

14. AROUND SLAD

Route: Painswick – The Frith – Furners Farm – Worgan's Farm – Sheephouse – Painswick

Distance: $5^1/_2$ miles

Map: O.S. Pathfinder 1113 Stroud

Start: The Falcon Inn, Painswick (Grid Reference: SO866097)

Access: The Falcon Inn is on the A46 in the centre of Painswick, just across the road from the church. It has a distinctive churchyard with lots of yew trees. There is a bus stop nearby, served by bus number 46 (Stroud – Cheltenham) on weekdays and number 23 (from Stroud) on Fridays only.

The Falcon Inn, Painswick (0452 812189)

A bowling green survives from the facilities of the original Falcon Inn, which was built around 1554 by the Jerningham family. They provided the Lords of the Manor of Painswick until 1804, but this didn't stop them indulging in cock-fighting. Mercifully, the old pub's cockpit has disappeared. It was still in use after the pub was rebuilt in 1711, during the reign of Queen Anne. There is a record of a cockmatch ". . . arranged between the Gentlemen of Painswick and the Gentlemen of Stroud to be fought on June 30th, 1731. They are to produce 24 cocks, ten of which they are obliged to fight for 2 guineas a battle and 10 guineas, the odd battle . . . ". Nowadays, cricket and football serve as pastimes. Today's pub has a friendly atmosphere, although it is said to be haunted by the ghost of a lady.

Accommodation is available, so you may discover for yourself if she would fancy visiting you during the night. Bar meals are also available, with vegetarians and vegans catered for. Uley Bitter is just one of the real ales you could sample. The opening hours are 12 noon to 3 p.m. daily and 6 p.m. to 11.30 p.m. on weekdays (not open on Sunday evenings).

The Falcon Inn, Painswick

Painswick

Affluence is in evidence everywhere, coupled with the skills that brought it to this place. Visit the Antiques and Craft Centre. This is also on the A46 (New Street) across the road from the Falcon Inn and between it and the Post Office. Housed within a tastefully converted Georgian chapel, it displays an interesting range of British handcrafted goods. Opening hours are 10 a.m. to 5 p.m. Monday to Friday, 9.30 a.m. to 5.30 p.m. on Saturday and 11 a.m. to 5.30 p.m. on Sunday.

This walk descends to pass Painswick Mill, which was valued at £110 in 1822. The decline in the local woollen industry reduced its value to £ 85 in 1838, despite the house being included. It was still working, as a silk mill, in 1960. The millpond has been cleaned recently and a new house has been built on the rise above it. Industry has departed, however. The British Army's scarlet uniforms used to be made here, with elderberry providing the scarlet dye.

As you return to Painswick at the end of the walk, notice the Elizabethan brickwork of Kingsmill. A cloth mill may have existed here since the 15th century. The owner went bankrupt in 1858, when the property comprised a ground floor, first and second floors, wool stores, drying stores, teasel house and other outbuildings with two excellent water-wheels driven by 'a never failing stream' (the millpond is fed by both the Painswick and Washbrook streams). By 1863, the property was a pin mill owned by John Cutch, John Williams & Co. Watkins and Okey moved here from Capp Mill soon afterwards. They needed larger premises and went on to invent a better pin and hairpin manufacturing process, using water power only. Pin making was a thriving industry in Gloucestershire in the late 19th century.

Laurie Lee, the poet and author, spent his childhood years in the village of Slad. He recalled them in his classic novel 'Cider with Rosie', so read the book before doing this walk. Frith Wood is an interesting nature reserve. Frith may be derived from the Welsh word "ffridd', meaning mountain pasture or Sheepwalk. This would be in keeping with the linguistic mix of this old frontier zone. It is, therefore, ironic to find that The Frith is now woodland.

Climbing past Worgan's Wood on the way back to Painswick, notice Folly Acres Conservation Area. This has been set up as a Rural Conservation and Organic Growing Study Centre to promote the organic management of the land. It also encourages the return of native flora and fauna alongside domestic animals and food growing. It consists of one acre of natural woodland and six acres of paddocks with a central fruit and vegetable growing area. This is a private centre with its own camp-site and log cabin accommodation planned (tel. R. Sanders 0453 766822 for details). Don't pick wild flowers and shrubs as you pass, keep dogs on the lead and stick to the marked path!

The Walk

With your back to the Falcon Inn and facing Painswick church, go right along the pavement of the A46. Pass the lychgate of the church on your left, then a car park, before turning left down Stamages Lane. Look for a grassy track on your left.

Painswick church

Turn left along the grassy track. Follow an iron fence on your right to a squeeze stile beside a gate ahead. Reach Knapp Lane and turn right downhill. Go ahead across a green when the road bears right. Cross the lower road and take a road ahead to pass a millpond on your left and the old Painswick Mill on your right.

Bear right along the signposted, muddy, track. Reach a fork and go left uphill (along Ticklestone Lane). This enclosed path passes the ruined Haunted House on your right, which should make it an interesting place for a midnight stroll.

Emerge over a stile into the corner of a field and go ahead with a hedge on your right. Continue over a squeeze stile beside a gate in the next corner and with a fence on your right in the next field. Go ahead over a wooden step stile beside a gate and take a rough, hedged, lane to a crossroads. Continue up the signposted path past a barn on your right to a stile ahead. Walk with a fence on your left to enter woodland at the next corner.

This wood is The Frith, a nature reserve. Follow the path across a track and ascend with it, as waymarked in blue. The path bears right as you climb. Come to a junction of forest tracks and bear left up the second

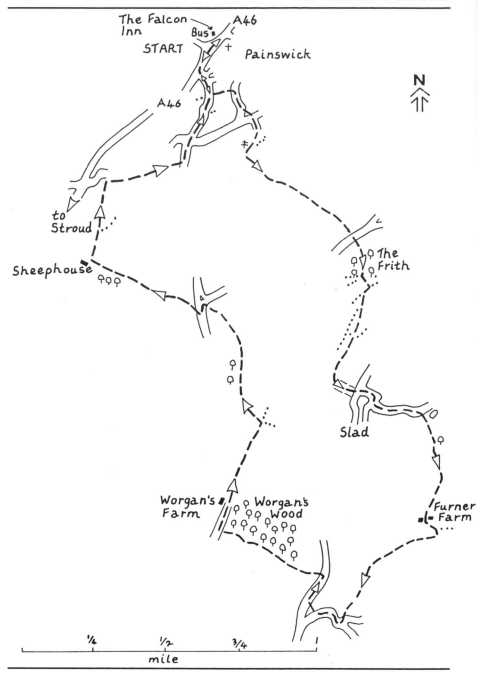

track from your left, for just 10 yards. Turn right up a narrow path, waymarked in blue. Emerge at a clearing and turn right for 50 yards, then take the signposted bridleway on your left. Waymarked in blue, this descends and bears right along a valley track. Go left at a fork and reach a lane.

Turn left down the lane to Slad War Memorial, near the bus stop for the number 23 (from and to Stroud). Cross the road and go down the lane opposite. Bend right to a junction and turn left down to a pool on your right. Turn right just before this pool to follow the path which passes it on your left. Cross a stile and go up the waymarked path running beside a hedge on your right.

Take a stile in the corner to enter a belt of trees and bear right, as waymarked by a yellow arrow. Emerge over a stile in the top right corner and follow the hedge on your left. Cross a stile beside the gate in the fence ahead. Keep beside the hedge on your left as you pass an orchard on your right.

Follow the track past farm buildings and bend left with it. Look out for a stile on your right. Bear right over it to descend as waymarked by a yellow arrow to another waymarked stile in the fence, which is on your right. Turn right over this to cross the foot of an old orchard to a stile in a fence ahead.

Veer left, as waymarked, down to a footbridge. Cross the stream and bear half-right up a pasture to a stile beside a gate in the top hedge. Admire the view over Slad on your right. Go ahead to cross a second stile within 10 yards and follow the path across the top of the field to a stile in the fence ahead, just above a row of trees.

Turn left along a track to join a road. Turn right down this, as signposted to The Vetch. Follow the road as it bends right. When it is about to bear left uphill, bear right over a stile beside a gate and follow the signposted path which climbs beside a fence on your right. Reach a stile in the top right corner and cross it to a road (the B4070).

Go right along the pavement. Pass Woodside House on your left, then turn left up a steep path. Join a track and keep climbing beside a wall on your left. Go ahead through a gate into a corner of a field and continue past Worgan's Wood on your right. Cross a stile to enter Folly Acres and walk with a wall on your right to Folly Lane.

Turn right along the lane, which soon deteriorates to a track. Turn left at a T-junction and walk with a wall on your left at first, then bear right across a field to descend gradually with the track to a road.

Turn left and keep left at a junction for 50 yards. Turn right through a gate and walk with a hedge on your left. Go through a gate in the corner ahead to follow a fence on your right in the next field. Continue through a squeeze stile and down a fenced path. Emerge through another squeeze stile to pass a house (Sheephouse) on your left and turn right along its access drive.

Fork left, downhill, to Kingsmill. Turn right over a waymarked footbridge across the stream. Go ahead across meadows, keeping the stream on your left. A hedged path leads past a private garden to a squeeze stile. Continue beside the stream on your left and a fence on your right to reach a road. Turn left up Stepping Stone Lane. Go ahead uphill at a crossroads to rejoin your outward route and retrace your steps to the start.

15. OAKRIDGE & SICCARIDGE WOOD

Route: Oakridge – Thames and Severn Canal – The Daneway Inn – Siccaridge Wood – Oakridge

Distance: 5 miles

Map: O.S. Pathfinder 1113 Stroud

Start: The Butchers Arms, Oakridge (Grid Reference: SP915037)

Access: The Butchers Arms stands back from the road, and there is a car park. The bus to Oakridge from Stroud via Bisley passes along here. There is a bus stop nearby and the bus service is No. 25 (weekdays only). This is fairly infrequent, so do check the times (tel. Stroud 763421). Stroud is the nearest railway station.

The Butchers Arms, Oakridge (0285-760371)

CAMRA named this as their Gloucestershire 'Pub of the Year' in 1991, so allow time to judge for yourself. Archers Best Bitter, Butcombe Bitter, Marston Burton Bitter and Uley Old Spot can all be sampled, while there are bar lunches. Evening meals are served in the Stable Room on Sunday lunchtimes (12 noon to 2 p.m.) and on Wednesday, Thursday, Friday and Saturday evenings (7.30 p.m. to 9.45 p.m.). Children have a small room and a large garden to play in. Opening hours are 12 noon to 3 p.m. and 6 p.m. to 11 p.m. on weekdays, 12 noon to 3 p.m. and 7 p.m. to 10.30 p.m. on Sundays. The only drawback is the pub's history (but, at least, it has changed for the better). This was a butchery and slaughterhouse in the 1760s and it was sold as a butcher's shop and brewerhouse in 1837.

The Daneway Inn (0285 760297)

No, this is not an old Viking watering-hole! It merely dates from 1784, when there was an invasion of Irish 'navvies', or navigators, to dig the

Thames and Severn Canal. John Nook, the canal's contractor, built it to house miners from the West Country and Derbyshire. Their expertise was needed to construct the nearby Sapperton Tunnel. The canal reached here in 1786 but the tunnel wasn't completed until 1789. During this time, this inn, which stands near the last of the 44 locks which raised the canal from Stroud to the level of the tunnel entrance, was a hive of activity.

The Thames and Severn Canal

Water-borne cargoes, such as stone, coal and timber, were off-loaded and carted to Cirencester. The inn's isolation helped to keep the Irish 'navvies, away from Sapperton village, where their behaviour was considered scandalous. Nevertheless, it seems that some local girls did marry, or go off with them. When the tunnel was open, the canal provided refreshment for the 'leggers'. Now it serves ramblers with real ale, bar meals and morning coffee. A no smoking area forms a small family room, while there is also a garden and a car park. Opening hours are 11 a.m. to 2.30 p.m. and 6.30 p.m. to 11 p.m. Mondays to Fridays; 11 a.m. to 3 p.m. and 6.30 p.m. to 11 p.m. on Saturdays; 12 noon to 3 p.m. and 7 p.m. to 10.30 p.m. on Sundays.

Oakridge

This small village stands above the steep slopes of the secluded valley of the River Frome. This was known as the Golden Valley in the early 19th century, when the local woollen industry boasted 150 mills.

The hillsides are still dotted with former weavers' cottages. The Thames and Severn Canal that was dug to serve the mills is now derelict, but an old feeder reservoir is passed. Its towpath makes for level, straightforward, walking. Returning through Siccaridge Wood, this Nature Reserve has a rich variety of wild flowers in May, while butterflies abound in the summer. Please heed the notices asking you not to pick the Lilies of the Valley. Back in the village, St Bartholomew's Church is worth a visit, even if it was only built as a chapel of ease for Bisley Church as recently as 1837. This was when Thomas Keble, brother of the John Keble who founded Keble College in Oxford, held the living. His energy raised £4000 to build this church in Early English style. On the south wall is a memorial to General Lord Robertson of Oakridge, 1896 – 1974, soldier, statesman and administrator. The Church of England school across the green was built in 1872 to replace a former National School which stood in the churchyard.

The Walk

From the car park of the Butchers Arms, go left down the road to the green, with the school on your right and the church on your left. Ignore a signposted path on your left after the church. Bear half-right to a stile beside a gate, waymarked with a yellow arrow, between houses. Cross this stile and turn left to continue over another stile beside a gate. Walk down the left-hand edge of a field to a stile beside a gate in the bottom left corner. Follow a wall on your left to a stile in the fence ahead and descend beside a hedge on your left before veering right to a stile in the fence ahead.

Cross the stile to enter woodland. Descend 30 yards, then turn left over a stile to descend more gradually. Keep left when a path joins yours from the right. Reach the bottom, where a sign proclaims Three Groves Wood Nature Reserve. Turn left along a lane. Go right at a fork towards Frampton Mansell, cross a bridge and bend left with the lane for 40 yards.

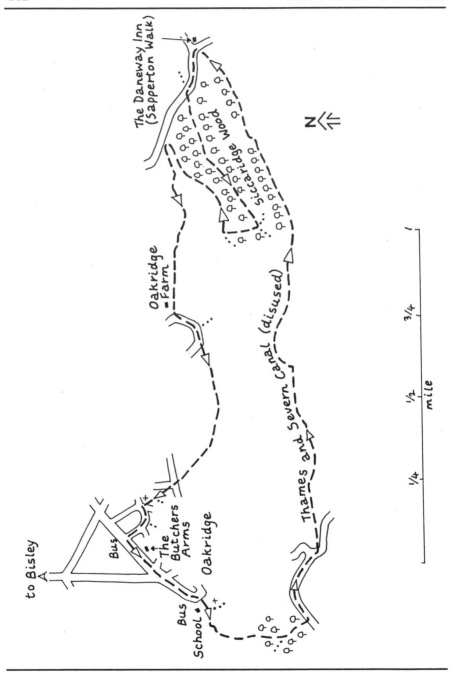

Turn left down steps and cross a footbridge at one of the old locks of the Thames and Severn Canal. Turn right to walk along the towpath. Simply follow the towpath all the way to the Daneway Inn. Be prepared to switch sides: first, when you turn right over a bridge to put the canal on your left. You then follow the towpath and pass under a brick bridge. After going past Siccaridge Wood, across the canal on your left, turn left over a wooden footbridge. You then turn immediately right to walk with the canal now on your right. Emerge at the Daneway Inn.

Fork left up the road towards Waterlane and Bisley. Reach a stile beside a signpost on your right, but don't cross it. Instead, turn left over a stile beside a gate to enter Siccaridge Wood Nature Reserve. Take the track ahead and do, please, observe the 'Please Do Not Pick the Lilies of the Valley – Leave them for others to enjoy' notices.

Reach a track junction and turn right downhill. Ignore a path on your left as you continue to descend rather steeply to the valley path at the foot of the trees. Turn right to follow this, walking with a fence (very soon becoming a hedge) on your left and trees on your right. Keep to this track through the trees to emerge over a stile beside a gate.

Turn sharply left along a stony track. After 50 yards, just before a house, turn left through a waymarked gap in the hedge. Turn right immediately to follow a path just inside the wood. Go ahead over a stile and follow a fence on your left. Descend to a wooden fence at the foot of the hill and turn left over a stone stile. Go ahead over a stone slab footbridge.

Cross the next field to take a stile into more woodland. Follow this path through the trees to emerge at a gate in the corner of a field. Bear half-right across this field to a metal gate and maintain your direction over the next field. Continue through a gate to the left of a metal barn and take a walled path to a lane.

Turn left along the lane, ignore a No Through Road ('Unsuitable for Motors') on your left at a junction. Keep right along the lane for 100 more yards, then take the squeeze stile beside the Waymarked gate in the corner ahead, as the lane bends right.

Go ahead beside a hedge on your left. Cross another squeeze stile in the corner at the end of a long field and head slightly right uphill to a gate.

Continue along the left and edge of a field. Use a squeeze stile beside a gate to reach a road.

Cross the road carefully to follow the lane ahead. Fork left after 25 yards along a walled track. Reach a Methodist church on your right at a crossroads. Turn left (but not sharply left) to take the level road which soon bends right to climb to the road used by the bus above the village. Turn left to head back to the pub.

The Butcher's Arms, Oakridge

16. SAPPERTON

Route: Sapperton – Pinbury Park – Edgeworth Manor – Tunley Cottage – The Daneway Inn – Thames and Severn Canal – Sapperton

Distance: $5^1/_2$ miles

Map: O.S. Pathfinder 1113 Stroud

Start: The Bell Inn, Sapperton (Grid Reference: SP948032)

Access: The Bell Inn stands in the village street at Sapperton, not far from the church. Between these two landmarks is the bus stop. There is an infrequent bus which connects Minchinhampton and Cirencester, run by Rover Coaches (tel. Nailsworth 2722). But you would be better off combining this walk with the one starting from Oakridge and making a long day of it between buses (no. 25) from Stroud to Oakridge. There is also bus no 23 from Stroud, which makes a rare appearance in Edgeworth, along this route (tel. Stroud 763421 for details). There is great satisfaction to be had from approaching the tenuous edge of the public transport network. You can beat the confounded timetable leaflets by devising an itinerary that will allow you to enjoy a walk! Using the current timetable (February, 1992), if you take the 9.30 a.m. bus number 23 from Stroud on a Friday ONLY, you could reach Edgeworth at 10.14 a.m. after a mini-tour of the Cotswolds. You could then walk this route and consume your pub lunch halfway round before catching the number 23 bus from Edgeworth at 2.01 p.m. on a Friday ONLY, to reach Stroud (with its railway station) at 2.45 p.m. There is also a bus (no 64 or 64A) from Stroud to Cirencester via Sapperton (tel Stroud 763421 for details).

The Bell Inn (0285 760298)

This is an old pub, full of character and the heart of the village. As such, it contrasts with the Daneway Inn which is also visited by this route and provides a link with the walk from Oakridge. Real ale is plentiful, while meals are available. There is a garden and a car park. Opening hours are 11 a.m. to 3 p.m. and 6 p.m. to 11 p.m. on weekdays, 12 noon to 3 p.m. and 7 p.m. to 10.30 p.m. on Sundays.

The Bell Inn

SAPPERTON

The village was the home of Ernest Gimson and Sydney and Ernest Barnsley, followers of William Morris and architects who were also renowned for designing beautiful furniture. Ernest Gimson died in 1919 aged 54 and lies buried in Sapperton churchyard. An interesting and beautiful account of the village during this period is 'By Chance I Did Rove' by Norman Jewson.

Set on the edge of the village above the valley is St Kenelm's Church. This saint had his shrine at Winchcombe Abbey. The present church dates mostly from the reign of Queen Anne, although it is on the site of a Norman church. Old oak panelling for it was brought from the manor house which used to stand on the north side of the church. This was demolished around the time that the first Earl Bathurst (of Cirencester Park) purchased the manor of Sapperton from the trustees of Sir Robert Atkyns the younger in 1730. Sir Robert, who resided at Pinbury Park, was known as the Gloucestershire historian. His wife, Louise, features (as a young girl) in Pepys' Diary.

A stone slab under the altar marks the burial place of Henry Wentworth, Major General to King Charles I. He died in 1644, the year that the king made a visit to the old manor house, described as 'the sweet brave seat of Sapperton'.

The charm of this little church has been added to by the attractive kneelers, depicting the rich natural history of the parish. They were the brain-child of the vicar's wife and Lady Marjorie Campbell, whose husband commanded the North Atlantic Convoys Protection Fleet in World War II. The organ stool cushion, designed by Lady Campbell, shows the young St Kenelm riding out on his white horse to be murdered in a trap laid by his jealous sister. Outside in the churchyard stand the mutilated remains of a medieval cross. Look for the grave of Rebekah Mason (died 1759). If you know enough about American history to recognise the Mason-Dixon line (separating the North from the South before the American Civil War), it is of interest to discover that her husband, a distinguished astronomer, was the Mason in the partnership.

Ernest Gimson and the Barnsley brothers made their names restoring Finbury Park for Lord Bathurst before they built cottages for themselves in Sapperton. Pinbury Park was also the home of the poet laureate, John Masefield, during World War II. Edgeworth's manor house is said to have been built on the site of a Roman villa. Its church is of Saxon origin, although it has been over-restored. There is a medieval cross in the churchyard.

The Walk

With your back to the Bell Inn, go right towards Sapperton's church and turn right to take the signposted bridleway behind the village telephone box. Cross the field to a small, waymarked, wooden gate. Go through it and turn left along an enclosed path.

Take a waymarked gate on your left to enter woodland. Go through a waymarked gate ahead and walk up a long, narrow, pasture between trees. When a track ascends to bear right, fork left and go ahead along a muddy track. Continue through a waymarked gate. Pass a belt of trees on your right and take the track over grass to a gate in a fence ahead.

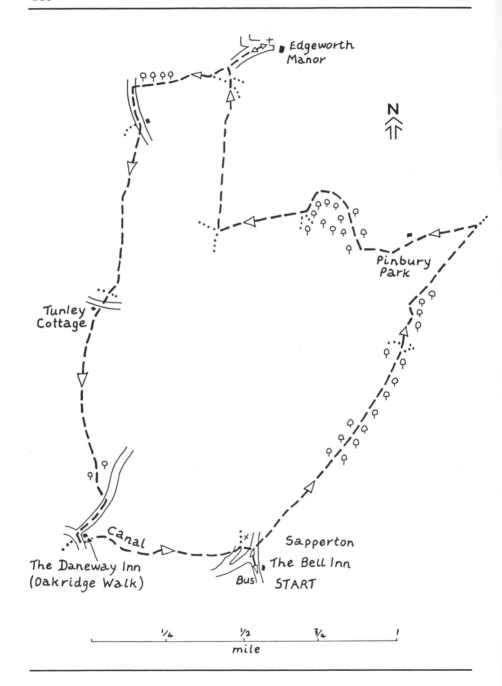

N

Edgeworth
Manor

Pinbury
Park

Tunley
Cottage

Canal

The Daneway Inn
(Oakridge Walk)

Bus

Sapperton
The Bell Inn
START

¼   ½   ¾   1
mile

Continue past a pond on your left. Turn sharply left at a junction with an access lane. Follow this to Pinbury Park, where there is a sign saying 'Please be so good as to send back our little dog who is probably following you at this moment'. Continue along a gravel track. This heads right into woodland. Take the wooden footbridge to the right of a ford and continue through a gate to walk beside the perimeter fence of the wood on your left. Go ahead through the next gate to follow a woodland track which climbs and bends left. Emerge at a gate on your right.

Bear right through the gate and follow the track along the right-hand edge of a field. Continue through a gate and turn right over a stile

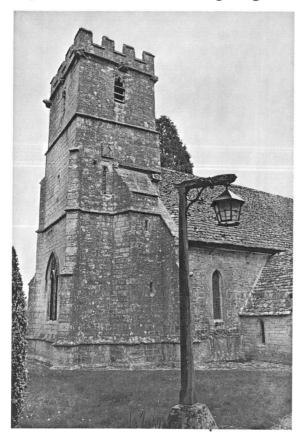

Edgeworth church

beside a small gate waymarked with a blue arrow. Follow a wall on your right. Take a small gate in the corner ahead and walk with an iron fence on your right. Go ahead through a small wooden gate in the next corner. Veer left, as waymarked by a blue arrow. Reach a cottage ahead.

Divert to Edgeworth Manor by turning right over a stone stile in a wall to the left of a gate and following the lane to Edgeworth Manor. Retrace your steps to the cottage you were facing before the stone stile. Facing it as before, go left i.e. go ahead when coming from Edgeworth Manor.

Pass the cottage garden fence on your right and cross the field to join a track.

Go ahead through a waymarked gate to walk with a hedge on your left and trees on your right. Emerge at a road and turn left, for 250 yards. Do not turn right along a signposted track with a gate across it, opposite farm buildings, but do bear right over a signposted stile shortly afterwards.

Cross the field as signposted, to a stile in the next fence. Head very slightly to the left as you follow the well-trodden path across the next field to a stile in the fence ahead. Cross this to walk beside a hedge on your left. Continue over a stile in the next corner.

Veer right to a gate at the bottom of the next field. Go ahead across a track and down to a stile which gives access to a lane near a house (Tunley Cottage). Cross the lane and take the signposted path to the left of the house. Continue through a small wooden gate at the back of the property and go ahead. A single stranded fence may be in place to guide you to the corner of a hedge.

Walk with the hedge on your right. Continue through a gate when you reach a corner. Follow the well-trodden path ahead which descends and bears right to a stile in a fence. Cross this and bear left over a second stile beside a gate. Go down a muddy track with a fence on your right and reach a road. Turn right to reach the Daneway Inn.

Go left across the bridge over the Thames and Severn Canal. Turn left along the route of the towpath past the car park of the Daneway Inn, which has been built over the site of the canal, on your left. Reach the mouth of the famous Sapperton Tunnel and follow the path across the top of it

Go ahead over a stile and veer right uphill over pasture. Cross a stile at the top and turn left to walk with a fence on your left. Reach a lane and go left towards St Kenelm's Church. Turn right before the church to take the metalled path uphill to a road. Pass the telephone box on your left to return to the Bell Inn, Sapperton.

17. NORTH OF CIRENCESTER

Route: Cirencester – Roman Amphitheatre – Cirencester Park – Stratton – Baunton – Bowling Green – Abbey Grounds – Cirencester.

Distance: 6 miles

Map: O.S. Pathfinder 1114 Cirencester

Start: The Brewers Arms, Cirencester (Grid Reference: SP024017)

Access: The buses stop in Market Place, where there is also one of several car parks in Cirencester. The Tourist Information Centre is here too. Facing the church of St. John the Baptist, go left and turn left up Cricklade Street. Pass Ashcroft Road on your right before coming to the Brewers Arms, also on your right. Cirencester can be reached by bus on weekdays from Cheltenham (nos. 51, X51 and X53) and Swindon (nos. 51, X51, X52, X53 and 77).

The Brewers Arms (0285 3763)

This busy town pub is famous for its lunch menu. Real ales are served, including BBB, Arkells Bitter and Kingsdown Ale. The opening hours are 11 a.m. to 3 p.m. and 6 p.m. to 11 p.m. on Monday and Friday; 11.30 a.m. to 3 p.m. and 7 p.m. to 11 p.m. on Tuesday, Wednesday and Thursday; Sunday hours are 12 noon to 3 p.m. and 7 p.m. to 10.30 p.m.

Cirencester

Cirencester basks in the glory of having been the second most important city in Roman Britain. It began as a small fort beside the Fosse Way where it crosses the River Churn. This soon moved northwards to firmer ground bounded by the modern Watermoor Road, St. Michael's Fields, Chester Street and The Avenue (11 to the south-east of The Brewers Arms and away from the present Market Place). The local Dubunni tribe had come to terms with the Romans and soon abandoned its centre at Bagendon, about three miles to the north, to settle beside the camp and trade with the soldiers. By AD 75 the fort was abandoned and demolished, to be replaced by a civil settlement.

The characteristic Roman pattern of a regular grid of streets was followed. Lewis Lane still conforms to this. A forum was laid out on the northern end of the space previously occupied by the fort, roughly at the modern Tower Street. This open market place had colonnades of shops on three sides and a basilica, or town hall, on the fourth. Constructed out of local stone, this was over 100 yards long and about 25 yards wide. Rows of open shops were protected only by Colonnades. Wealthier people lived in more elaborate houses which stood in their own grounds further out.

All this was defended by two miles of fortifications. The River Churn was canalised through an outer ditch overlooked by an earth bank. Monumental gateways were built to each of the town's four main entrances. A stone wall was then built into the front of the rampart. Later, external bastions were built at intervals along the walls. These were lavish defences and enclosed some 240 acres. Only London was bigger in Roman times. The Romans inspired this urbanisation, but the local British tribe, the Dobunni quickly adopted the town as their administrative centre. They obviously shared the Roman enthusiasm for 'sports' such as gladiatorial combats. During the second century AD an amphitheatre was built on the western edge of the town. Visiting it today brings views of impressively high grassy banks in an oval which seems to be a mini-Wembley. Archaeologists are sure that it was first built with timber and earth, then revetted with stone. Terraces of low limestone walls probably supported wooden seats. The capacity was in the region of seven or eight thousand.

Christianity had its place in Corinium Dobunnorum too. The famous word square or acrostic containing a Christian message 'A (for Alpha) Pater Noster O (for Omega)' was found scratched on the wall of one Roman house. An important route centre, with Ermin Street meeting Akeman Street, the Fosse Way and other Roman roads here, the town survived until the decisive Battle of Durham in 577 delivered what was to become England to the Saxons.

The conquerors were suspicious of towns and when markets did return here they were held in the Market Place, well to the north of the old forum. The establishment of the now ruined Abbey of St Mary here brought a revival in the Middle Ages. By the time Henry VIII dissolved it the wool trade had brought new wealth to Cirencester. The best place to find out about the town's fascinating history is the Corinium Museum, which is reckoned to be one of the top twenty museums in the country. Exhibits include a splendid collection of Roman mosaics. The museum is open daily except Monday from November to March and Christmas Day, Boxing Day and New Year's Day. Opening hours are 10 a.m. to 5 p.m. (5.30 p.m. in the summer) on weekdays and 2 p.m. to 5 p.m. (5.30 p.m. in the summer) on Sundays.

Abbey grounds gatehouse

Bearing in mind Cirencester's proximity to the frontier between King Arthur's Britain and the land occupied by the Saxons in the sixth century, it is interesting to note that the oldest pub in Cirencester is the Black Horse Inn, near the Market Place and on the corner of Cricklade Street and Castle Street. A very interesting thesis put forward by S.G. Wildman in his book 'The Black Horsemen' (published by John Baker in 1971) links these pubs with the watering-holes frequented by King

Arthur's 'knights' on their frontier patrols, riding black horses, like the ones that were stationed on Hadrian's Wall. There might even be a wall picture of one of Arthur's Black Horsemen at North Cerney church, some five miles north of Cirencester.

Cirencester Park

This route gives you the opportunity to extend your walk into Cirencester Park. Notices at the entrance welcome you – on foot and unaccompanied by a dog – with the permission of the Earl Bathurst. If you have the time, do wander in this parkland. The Broad Ride stretched nearly five miles westwards, almost to Sapperton. Please remember that you walk here as a privileged guest, however, and take your litter home.

The Walk

The Brewers Arms

With your back to The Brewers Arms, go right to a crossroads and turn right along Queens Lane. This is on the line of the old Roman street out of town to the amphitheatre. Nowadays, it's necessary to turn left up Querns Hill, take the bridge across the Bristol Road and fork right up Cotswold Avenue. Turn right through a small wooden gate beside a fieldgate to cross the grass and inspect the huge bowl of the Roman amphitheatre. This is known locally as the Bull Ring. Retrace your steps to The Brewers Arms.

Continue up Cricklade Street, passing The Brewers Arms on your left. Reach Market Place, whose odd shape is definitely

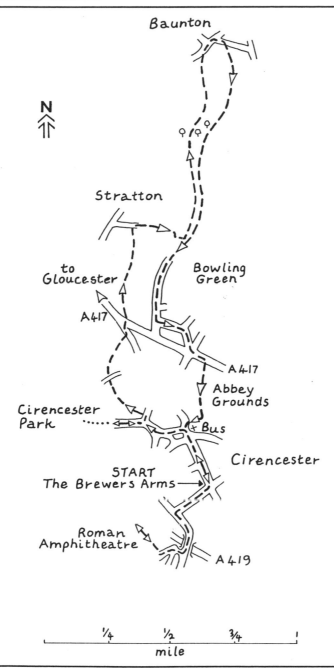

Baunton

N

Stratton

to
Gloucester

A417

Bowling
Green

A417

Abbey
Grounds

Cirencester
Park

Bus

Cirencester

START
The Brewers Arms

Roman
Amphitheatre

A419

¼ ½ ¾
mile

medieval, not Roman! Go ahead up West Market Place and turn left along Black Jack Street. This leads to the Corinium Museum, on your right, and Park Street. Bear right up this, noticing the 40ft yew hedge (reputedly the highest in Europe) which rises behind the Earl Bathurst's mansion, on your left.

Divert left up Cecily Hill, leaving the 240 acres enclosed by the Roman city wall. The hill derived its name from a long-gone chapel dedicated to St Cecelia. It was the main road to Stroud until the early 19th century. Now it leads to the Earl Bathurst's Cirencester Park, where you have permission to walk. This 3000 acre estate was designed by Alexander Pope. Turning round, downhill, pass the old barracks for the Royal North Gloucestershire Militia on your left.

At the foot of the hill, turn left and very soon turn left again to follow the signposted Riverside Walk. This follows the old Mill Pound on your left and veers right to cross Barton Lane. Bear slightly right to continue over a footbridge and walk beside the river on your right. Reach Gloucester Street and turn left to the A417. Turn right to cross this carefully and take a stile into a meadow.

Follow the path towards Stratton, crossing the meadow to a stile at the right-hand end of the wall ahead. Continue with the River Churn on your right. Pass tennis courts with floodlights on your left, cross a stile ahead and follow a wall on your right. Reach a road and turn right to pass West Midland Farmers on your left. Cross a stile at the end of the road and continue over a stone slab footbridge and over a meadow to a footbridge near a cottage.

Cross the second footbridge and go right to pass the cottage on your left, then turn left over a stile and go along a paved path. Turn left and immediately cross a stile waymarked with a yellow arrow just to the right of a lower gate. Go ahead beside a hedge on your right. Take the gate in the corner into the next field and follow the hedge on your right until it veers away to the right. Go straight ahead instead, across the field to a copse.

Cross a waymarked stile to enter the copse. Bear right between the trees and turn left when a yellow arrow on a tree points to a stone stile in the perimeter fence. Start beside a hedge on your left and continue to a waymarked stile to the right of a gate in the wall ahead. Cross the next field and take the waymarked gate to follow a wall on your right to a gate giving access to a lane.

Go right at a junction and go right again at a fork to pass 'Stonecroft' on your left. Follow the lane through a gate ahead and go with it as it bends right, with a wall on your right. Turn right through a gate waymarked with a blue arrow and keep beside the wall on your right. The bridleway goes ahead through a gate to be enclosed by a fence on your left and the wall on your right. This soon becomes a hedge on your right. Keep to it as you pass fields on your left. Eventually emerge through a gate to pass the lower gate and stile, now on your right, which you used on your outward journey.

Take the clear track ahead. This turns into a road with a pavement (Bowling Green Lane). Pass Bowling Green Road on your left, but turn left up Shepherds Way Fork right down St John's Road to the A417. Cross the A417 with care and go left until you see the Norman Arch of the old Abbey gate-house on your right. Turn right through this into the grounds of the old (12th century) Augustinian abbey. Follow the path ahead towards the tower of St John's Church, passing an attractive lake on your left. Reach a T-junction in the far corner. Divert left if you wish to inspect part of the old Roman wall. Go right to emerge past the church onto Market Place. Cricklade Street is ahead, with The Brewers Arms near the bottom of it on your left.

18. HETTY PEGLER'S TUMP

Route: The Old Crown Inn, Uley – Toney Wood – Hetty Pegler's Tump – Uley Bury Hillfort – The Old Crown Inn, Uley

Distance: 5 miles

Maps: O.S. Pathfinders 1112 Frampton on Severn and 1132 Dursley.

Start: The Old Crown Inn, Uley (Grid Reference: ST792986)

Access: The Old Crown Inn is in the centre of Uley, which is on the B4066 between Stroud (the nearest railway station) and Dursley. There is a car park at the pub, while the village bus stop is nearby. A good weekday service (no. 15) runs from Stroud and Dursley.

The Old Crown Inn (0453 860502)

Uley Bitter, the locally brewed, well-hopped and malty real ale, is served in this attractive 17th century building that began life as a farm cottage. There is a beer garden, a children's room, a range of bar meals, and a friendly atmosphere. Why not make this your touring base? En suite bed and breakfast accommodation is available. Opening hours are 11.30 a.m. to 2.30 p.m. and 7 p.m. to 11 p.m. on weekdays; noon to 2.30 p.m. and 7 p.m. to 10.30 p.m. on Sundays.

Uley

This is a special place swirling in the mists of time above the Severn estuary. Sacred pathways meet here and whatever leys are (some think they are channels for spiritual energy) they appear to meet at Uley. The very place-name suggests so, with the U a possible reference to the yew trees to which leys often gravitate in ancient churchyards. Two sites (Hetty Pegler's Tump and Uley Bury Hillfort) are visited on this walk. Religious rites and ceremonies have been performed here for at least 4000 years. Men laying a pipeline in 1979 dug up a Romano-British temple of the fourth century and the magnificent limestone head of a seven-foot high broken statue of Mercury – the God of pathways whose 'mark' is a standing stone.

A simple Christian church appears to have replaced Mercury's temple in the fifth century, on Crawley Hill just to the north of the present church. The Normans built St Giles' church, near the start of this walk, and the first rector of it to have his name recorded for posterity was Osmund, in 1180. Prosperity came to the village in the 18th century, when the fame of 'Uley Blue' cloth grew. Eighteen mills manufactured the fine, broad cloth. The workers were served by 11 pubs, which were condemned as 'seminaries of vice' and the cause of 'idleness and debauchery'. By the time that the woollen magnate Edward Shepherd (the builder of Princess Anne's home, Gatcombe House) went bankrupt in 1837, many had emigrated to Australia or Canada.

The church was rebuilt by the Victorians. It retained its dedication to St Giles, whose day is 1st September. This is the time of feasts and markets (and of St Giles' fair in Oxford) and markets are another function of Mercury. The 'Uley Feast' still takes place on St Giles' Day. No doubt this is an event of great antiquity.

Hetty Pegler's Tump

The detour to this ancient monument is well worthwhile. This is a chambered long barrow, dating back to the New Stone Age (at least 2000 BC). Its curious name is derived from Hester Pegler (died 1694) who was the wife of the owner (William Pegler, died 1695) of the field in which it stands. Workmen excavated it by accident in 1821 when they were digging for material to build the nearby road. They broke into the north-east burial chamber, destroying it. The north-west chamber has also been lost but the two southern chambers have survived.

There is also a fifth chamber at the western end of the passage. Dry-stone walling fills in the gaps between the large slabs of stone which form the walls. Fifteen skeletons were found here in 1821. Eight or nine more were found in 1854 and two human skeletons plus a quantity of wild boar jaw bones, suggesting roast pork on the menu, were found outside the entrance.

A much later burial with three fourth century Roman coins, was also found in the mound covering the cairn. Admission is free at any reasonable time, but you'll need the key to venture inside. This can be a memorable experience, especially when the annual ley hunters' moot chose to come here in 1989. Dowser Bill Lewis' pendulum suggested a much earlier date for the monument. Call at Crawley Hill Farm (second house on the right on the way to Uley) for the key. There is a small charge for this, while a torch is essential.

Hetty Pegler's Tump

Uley Bury Hillfort

This is the finest example of an Iron Age hillfort in the Cotswolds. Its interior area of 32 acres is defended by two banks and ditches. The ground falls away steeply on all of its four sides, except for a neck in its northern corner. Excavations have not taken place here, but a gold stater of the Dobunni, the local British tribe, has been ploughed up. Perhaps its greatest treasure is the range of spectacular views. One side takes in the Brecon Beacons and the Severn estuary beyond the distinctive bulk of

Cam Long Down and the tree-capped Downham Hill to the west. Turning the corner brings a fine view over the village of Uley. Its church acts as a prominent marker for the steep final descent.

The Walk

Go right to pass the village green on your right. Follow the B4066 towards Stroud to where it bends left up Crawley Hill. Fork right from it here by taking the rough track towards Mutterall Farm.

Reach the first house on your left and turn left past a garage to a stile. Go ahead over it and straight across a field which may be divided by a temporary fence with a stile in it. Continue over a stile beside a gate to the next field and maintain your direction to another stile beside a gate. After crossing this, bear right towards a stream (with frisky bullocks in close attendance – no doubt they were here to scare my wife when I first walked this way in about 1974, and their later incarnations greeted me as if I'd never left in 1991 – my wife chose to stay at home this time).

Cross a footbridge to say farewell to our friends who have only the butcher to look forward to. Turn left to walk uphill beside a stream on your left. Cross a stile and keep near the stream on your left as you go up the valley towards woodland. Approaching the top, look for a stile in the perimeter fence of Toney Wood, on your left. Cross it and turn right to climb to the top of the wood.

Go ahead to a stone stile beside a signpost and reach a road. Go left and ignore a turning to Nympsfield on your right. Reach the B4066 and turn left along its verge, towards Uley. Look for a path bearing downhill into the woodland on your right and signposted as the 'Cotswold Way'. You will return to take it, but first continue along the road to a brown English Heritage sign which points to 'Uley Long Barrow' on your right. This is Hetty Pegler's Tump and you can see it across the field. Follow the footpath to it (walking beside the hedge on your right).

Retrace your steps to the Cotswold Way signpost, now on your left. Go down the well-established path through the trees. Ignore side paths to reach a lane at the bottom. Turn left at a signpost and start to climb back up through the wood, following waymarks with the distinctive white dot of the Cotswold Way.

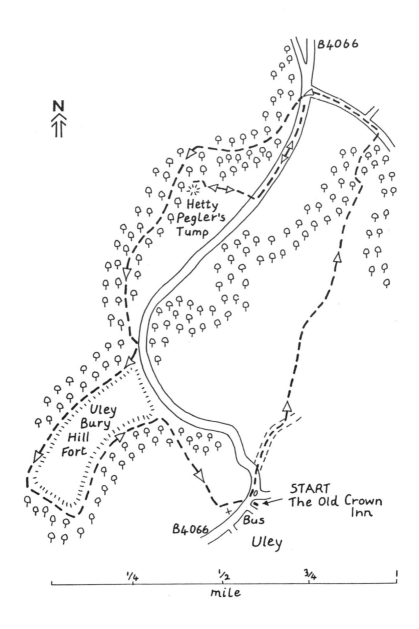

This woodland section of probably England's finest long distance path provides splendid views over the Severn estuary on your right. Late autumn is probably the best time to enjoy it, when the leaves are off the trees and form a golden-brown carpet. Eventually, reach a road. Turn right up the signposted public bridleway.

Bear right through a small gate beside a cattle grid which may be obscured by plant growth. Follow the stimulating path all around three sides of Uley Bury hillfort. When you turn the corner to the third side, you should gain a fine view of the modern village of Uley.

The Old Crown, Uley

In the fourth corner of the hillfort promenade, turn sharply right to descend along a signposted public bridleway. Soon leave it on your left by crossing a stile beside a gate to enter woodland. Follow a woodland path down to a small wooden gate.

Continue along a grassy slope with the wood on your left. Descend towards the church. As you approach the church, cross a wooden step stile in the fence just to the right of it. Go down an enclosed path. At the path junction, turn left beside the churchyard wall to pass the church on your right and reach the road. Cross the B4066 carefully to return to the Old Crown Inn, which is on your left.

19. NAILSWORTH AND AVENING

Route: The Weighbridge Inn – Nailsworth – Tipputs Inn – Ledgemore Bottom – Avening – The Weighbridge Inn

Distance: 8 miles

Map: O.S. Pathfinder 1133 Nailsworth and Tetbury

Start: The Weighbridge Inn (Grid Reference: ST862993)

Access: The Weighbridge Inn is beside the B4014 road between Nailsworth and Avening. This links with the A46 at Nailsworth, about four miles south of Stroud, the nearest railway station. There is a good weekday bus service from Stroud to the start of this walk (No. 31). A few buses start from Gloucester and all turn round at Tetbury. There is a car park at the start too.

The Weighbridge Inn (0453 832520)

The Weighbridge Inn's name reflects the connection between this valley and the cloth industry. Local wool provided the raw material, while water was harnessed for power. Mills, millponds and, no doubt, this inn, were built in the early 19th century. Today, the mills have gone but the inn remains to cater for walkers in some of the most attractive scenery of the Cotswolds. Real ale is served, including Wadworth, there are bar snacks and children are welcome. The opening hours are 11 a.m. to 2.30 p.m. and 7 p.m. to 11 p.m. on weekdays (6.30 p.m. start on Saturday evenings). Sunday opening hours are noon to 2.30 p.m. and 7 p.m. to 10.30 p.m.

The Woollen Mills

The deep valley at the start of this walk contains a woollen mill whose large mill pond ensured a reliable supply of water-power and enabled it to continue producing heavy woollen cloth from the early 19th century until the late 20th. Longford's Mill closed in 1990. Its pond covered 15 acres and cost £1000 to construct. There were dozens of other mills in this area until the Industrial Revolution centred the industry on Bradford (in West Yorkshire). If the Cotswolds had boasted the fast-flowing streams of the Pennines, the industry could have lingered on here.

The Weighbridge Inn

Nailsworth

This town was a creation of the cloth industry. Its parish dates from only 1895, when it was created out of Horsley, Avening and Amberley. St George's parish church wasn't built until 1900 but it now contains a mural on the west wall showing the life of the town. The Quakers were here in the 17th century and their Meeting House is still used. There were about 40 mills here in the early 19th century. Going up the side valley towards Horsley, this walk passes Ruskin Mill, complete with waterwheel and ducks on the mill pond. A cornmill occupied this site in the 16th century. By the early 17th century, there were 40 weavers in this part. Whole families worked together at home using hand looms. This was a favoured spot because it was at the edge of the plateau.

Avening

The open upland provides a contrast to the valley. The underlying limestone causes rain to drain away rapidly and Ledgemore Bottom is a fine example of a dry valley. Sheep have grazed here for centuries, although the native broadleaved trees (as opposed to exotic conifers) of the woodland encountered both here and above the start of this walk have a longer pedigree. Visit the Church of the Holy Cross in Avening. This is of the early Norman period, being dedicated on 14th September (Holy Cross Day), 1080. It also has a cruciform shape. Does this mark where what some dowsers recognise as male and female energy lines cross? The famous Dragon Line from Land's End via Glastonbury Tor and Avebury to the Norfolk coast appears to have a male line passing through churches dedicated to St Michael and a female line through churches dedicated to St Mary. Where they cross, as at the Church of the Holy Cross in Crediton, Devon, the dedication recognises that fact.

Notice the monument to Henry Brydges, kneeling at a prayer desk, in the north transept chapel. He has a lot to repent for, having been a pirate. As you climb out of Avening, look north

Avening church

across the valley to Gatcombe Park. Princess Anne, the Princess Royal, lives there now. Thousands of years ago our ancestors erected the Tingle Stone nearby. One of several standing stones in this area, it is beside a Neolithic long barrow and its name may come from tingling sensations or mild electric shocks felt by some people at certain times when touching it. Magnetic anomalies have also been found here. The name may also be derived from the old Norse word 'ting'. This means an assembly, as with Tynwald Hill on the Isle of Man. Such stones did serve as meeting-places in the past. If you try to touch it today, you'll get more than a gentle shock, however. Despite the nearby Steps Lane being a right of way, the Tingle Stone stands in a field belonging to Princess Anne. As a result, it is under constant surveillance by the security staff. If you really must have a feel of it, come when the annual horse trials are held and it may be possible to get to the stone.

The Walk

With your back to the Weighbridge Inn, go left along the road towards Nailsworth. After 200 yards, fork left up a track which has its signpost where there is space across the road. Continue near the right-hand edge of a field, descend into woodland and bear left into a side valley. Cross a stile and take a small footbridge over a stream to bear right just within the wood. Emerge in the corner of a field and follow the fence on your right to join a bridleway at a signpost. Turn right down it and through a gate.

Shortly after the gate, take the path on your left to walk between hedges down to Park Road. Turn left along this to the A46. Go left, then fork right along Old Bristol Road to pass Nailsworth Town Hall on your right. Notice a Gloucestershire County Council sign beyond the Town Hall and take the descending path on your right. Go left at the junction with a lower path, known as Arnolds Lane. Follow it back to the Old Bristol Road. Maintain your direction along this for 20 yards, then bear left on a path which ascends from the road.

Fork right after 30 yards to walk parallel to the road, which is below you. Follow this path down to Ruskin Mill, on your right. Go ahead to walk beside the millpond, on your right. Climb towards houses at its end and take the steps on your left to a lane, which you turn right along.

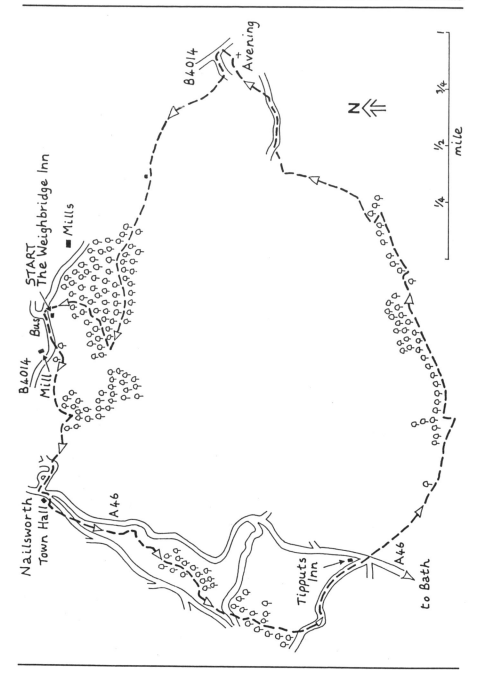

Walk around a bend to the left, then another to the right. When the lane bends left again, veer right on a level path which leads to a stile giving entry to a field.

Walk beside a fence on your right and cross a stile ahead into a second field. Veer away from the fence to reach a stone stile which you cross to follow a woodland path. This descends to take you across a stream. Go left along an access lane beside the stream. Continue to a road (going to Horsley on your right).

Cross the road to take the track ahead. Fork left after 100 yards to follow the fainter path which climbs through trees and becomes more obvious as it leads to a stile giving access to a field. Go ahead to pass a small electricity pylon and descend to a road (Hay Lane). Go left along it to reach Tipputs Inn.

Cross the A46 with care and go ahead along a track. Walk straight ahead along this, ignoring a fork to the left. Keep to the right-hand edge of two fields, then walk with trees (behind a fence on your left) in a third field. Go ahead to reach a concrete farm road.

Go left along the road through a gate and downhill for 100 yards. Turn right to walk with woodland on your left along the dry valley of Ledgemore Bottom. The long field leads to a wall. Go ahead through a gate in it and continue with the wood on your left to cross a stile to the right of a gate ahead.

Continue just to the left of the valley bottom, diverging from the fence which veers right. Walk with the perimeter fence of a patch of woodland on your right. Turn right to cross a stream and take a gate into another field.

Turn left to follow the perimeter fence (becoming a wall) of the wood on your left. Go left at its end to take a gate into the next field and go back across the stream. Turn right to go through another gate in a projecting corner of a field. Walk with a fence on your right to a stile in the next corner. Continue through a young plantation of trees and leave by the stile at its end.

Continue through a gate at the bottom right corner of this field. Reach a stile next to a gate into a small enclosure, cross it and the stone footbridge beside a ford. Another stile beside a gate leads to a walled track which brings you to a road.

Go right along the road for over 300 yards. Look out for a stile just before a house on your left. Turn left across it and descend past a garden on your right. Turn right through a small wooden gate to reach a paddock. Walk with a fence on your right to a stile giving access to a second paddock. Bear left downhill to a stile in the bottom corner. Go ahead to an enclosure, ignoring a path crossing the stream on your left. Walk with a fence on your left and through a waymarked kissing gate in the far corner. Head slightly right uphill to a stile in the next corner. Walk between stone walls towards Avening church, on your right.

Continue along the path to a road and reach the B4014 in the centre of Avening. Turn left along it towards Nailsworth. Turn left immediately after a garage to follow Woodstock Lane to a fork. Bear right along an unmetalled track and climb to a second fork where you go right again. A level track leads into a barn-yard. Take the footpath just to the right of this and stop to admire the view of Gatcombe Park on your right.

Cross a field to the buildings of Longman's Barn and follow the track to pass them on your right. Maintain your direction to enter woodland. Fork right along a bridleway between the trees. Follow the waymarks to a T-junction with a bridleway and a barrier to a path ahead. This is where you turn right to descend through the trees to a metal gate at the foot of the wood. Go through it into a field and descend. The right of way takes the course of what may be a stream near the bottom of the field. This old sunken way brings you to a small gate. Go through it to the B4014 and turn left to the Weighbridge Inn.

20. THAMES HEAD

Route: The Tavern, Kemble – Thames Head – Thames and Severn Canal – The Tunnel House – Tarlton – The Tavern, Kemble.

Distance: 7 miles

Maps: O.S. Pathfinders 1113 Stroud and 1133 Nailsworth

Start: The Tavern, Kemble (Grid Reference: ST985975)

Access: The Tavern is opposite Kemble's British Rail station, on the line between Swindon and Gloucester. There is also a weekday bus service from Cirencester and Tetbury (no. A1). There is a good Sunday train service. Cars can also be parked here.

The Tavern (0285 770216)

Kemble didn't have a public house for centuries until the Tavern opened its doors in 1946. It was previously the Coffee Tavern, reflecting the wishes of the local landowner and temperance M.P. Robert Gordon. He had also objected to the building of a proper station at this former railway junction.

Matters changed when a director of the Cheltenham and Great Western Union Railway Company had to change here in a draughty shed in winter, on the way to one of Lord Bathurst's Hunt Balls at Cirencester. He secured an Act of Parliament, with provisions for the company to buy land on the Gordon estate. This enabled a proper station to be built. Non-alcoholic and low-alcohol drinks are still available, while Arkells real ale is also served. A nine-hole putting green is open during the summer, while there is a playground for children, a beer garden, a skittle alley and billiards. Food is available and the opening hours are 11 a.m. to 2.30 p.m. and 6 p.m. to 11 p.m. on weekdays. Sunday opening hours are noon to 2 p.m. and 7 p.m. to 10.30 p.m.

The Tunnel House

The Tunnel House (0285 770280)

If you need refreshment half-way round this route, this pub is open daily 11 a.m. to 3 p.m. and 6.30 p.m. to 11 p.m. Real ale and food are served, while children are welcome. Built to serve the nearby Thames and Severn Canal, it is convenient for the mouth of the Sapperton Tunnel, from where boat trips may be available.

Thames Head

A simple stone block under an ash tree marks the official source of the longest river to run wholly within England. The Thames flows for about 210 miles to reach the sea (the 220 mile long River Severn, rises in Wales). Unless there is a miracle, you won't see it flowing here, in Trewsbury Mead, however. At most, you'll find a muddy depression. You'll have to check the field south of the Fosse Way for some actual water, so be aware of this as you walk from Kemble. John Leland faced the same problem when he came this way during Henry VIII's reign, although he called this the 'head of Isis'. The Ordnance Survey still state 'River Thames or Isis', on their pathfinder map. Furthermore, some claim that Seven Springs, south of Cheltenham, is the real source of the Thames. A debate in the House of Commons on 26th February 1937, was needed to settle the question.

Although further from the sea, Seven Springs is the source of the River Churn, a tributary of the Thames and with a name of great antiquity. Thames Head is the official source, but what of the Isis? Here we have a dim remembrance of times past, of a magical era when rivers were deemed to be alive and names were carefully chosen to denote meanings. Only a dreamy old place like Oxford would have even a vague recollection of this. Today's reserve rowing eight for Oxford University Boat Club is called Isis, as is the university journal. The River Thames is the Isis all the way to its confluence with the River Thame at Dorchester, an ancient sacred spot of great interest but outside the territory of this book (see 'Pub Walks in Oxfordshire').

It should be recorded, however, that Isis could refer to the mother goddess, while the Thame is the father god. When the female and male waters mingle, below the Wittenham Clumps, the River Thamesis is formed, being our Thames. All this is dismissed as the fancy of some 'medieval scribe', (J. R. L. Anderson, 'The Upper Thames', Eyre Methuen, 1974) but other opinions may differ.

The Thames and Severn Canal

Britain's principal rivers were joined in 1789 by the completion of this waterway. It linked the navigable Thames at Inglesham, near Lechlade, with Stroud, where the Stroudwater Canal provided the link to the Severn at Framilode. It seemed a sensible proposition, but failed, along with the local cloth industry that was meant to use it. When there was talk of turning it into a railway, the Great Western Railway bought it up in 1882 to prevent competition. The last traffic was in 1911 and the canal was officially abandoned in 1927. It suffered early on from competing canals, such as from Oxford to the Midlands.

One can only have sympathy with the visionaries trying to restore this route, however. Sapperton Tunnel is 3,817 yards long and deserves to be used. This walk passes its classical eastern portal, from where there may be boat trips along a restored section of the canal (tel. 0242 515181, 0672 513400 or 0666 502797 for details). This was the biggest tunnel of the 18th century. Its lining is a mixture of rough hewn natural rock and brick. The towpath does not go through it, while experts reckon it would have been too big and irregular to leg boats through. Poles probably did the job. At least the old canal towpath provides a fine footpath from near Thames Head to the Tunnel House. Shortly after passing under the bridge which carries the railway across the line of the canal, notice the ruin of one of the 'round houses' which were built to house the canal's maintenance men.

Kemble

This village grew with the coming of the railway in the 19th century. All around are more ancient sites, such as the Roman town of Cirencester and the lost medieval village of Hullasey, south of Tarlton. Trains still stop at Kemble, following the line of Isambard Kingdom Brunel's railway, even if this is now at standard gauge rather than with the rails 7' $1/_4$" apart. The branch lines to Cirencester and to Tetbury were both closed in 1964. In the 1920s, the world's fastest scheduled steam train service, the famous 'Cheltenham Flyer' came through here. 'The Cheltenham Spa Express' (now a high speed diesel) still calls.

The Walk

Go up the station approach and turn left across the bridge over the railway. Follow Station Road into the village and turn left at a T-junction. Walk north, out of the village and across the now filled-in line of the dismantled railway to Cirencester. Reach a stile beside a gate on your right and turn right over it to follow the signposted path.

Gradually veer right to a stile to the right of a gate in the next corner. Follow a track ahead, keeping a fence on your right, until it is about to bend right towards a road. Turn left to cross a footbridge and walk with the infant River Thames on your right. Keep an eye on the water as it will disappear soon. The right of way doesn't help you see the first drops of the Thames, as it veers left away from the river to a metal fieldgate in the far corner ahead.

Go ahead as signposted, keeping beside the hedge on your left. Notice a hedge coming in at a right angle on the far side of the hedge on your left. This marks where the right of way veers right across the field to a tall roadside signpost beside stone steps leading to a stile. The signpost gives Kemble as the path's destination, but it might as well state London, for this is part of the 175 mile Thames Walk from the source to the Thames Barrier. Look for weary backpackers.

Cross the road (the A433 and the old Roman Fosse Way) carefully and take a farm track ahead (using a stile to the right of the fieldgate). Cross the solidly-built ladder stile to the right of the gate in the wall ahead.

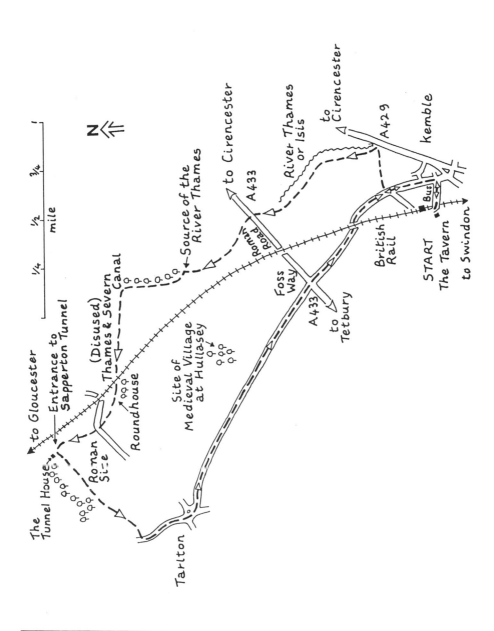

Head right beside a fragmented line of trees to a wooden step-stile beside a metal fieldgate. Maintain your direction to the stone marking the source of the River Thames.

Walk with trees on your right to a waymarked stile, beside a gate in the next corner. Continue with the perimeter fence of the woodland on your right. Cross another ladder stile, to the right of the gate in the next corner. Near the end of the woodland on your right, go ahead over a ladder stile beside a gate to follow a muddy track.

Approach an old stone bridge and go left just before it to follow the old bed of the Thames and Severn Canal on your right. Continue under the bridge carrying the railway over the canal and pass a ruined canal 'round house' on your left. Go ahead along the old towpath under a road bridge and with water in the canal on your right now. Reach the mouth of Sapperton Tunnel. Follow the path up steps to the Tunnel House.

Facing the Tunnel House, turn sharply left to a signposted gap in a wall. Veer right across fields (passing the site of a Roman settlement on your left). Cross a stone stile in the corner and walk with a wall on your right (ignoring inviting paths into Hailey Wood). When the wall bears right, veer left across the field until the wall turns and rejoins your path. Continue over a stone stile in the next corner. Bear right to pass farm buildings on your right and reach a gate beside a signpost. Go through it to a lane.

Turn left to reach a crossroads in Tarlton. Veer left along the road signposted for Kemble. In the absence of convenient footpaths, this is the return route to the village. Fortunately, there isn't much traffic, while a patch of woodland on your left suggests the site of the lost medieval village of Hullasey. Many such villages were abandoned in the days of the Black Death and other plagues.

Take care when crossing the A433. In Roman times, this was the Fosse Way between Exeter and Lincoln, via Bath and Cirencester. Continue along the road ahead into Kemble and retrace your steps up Station Road to the Tavern.

21. THE COTSWOLD WATER PARK

Route: Cerney Wick – Old Railway – South Cerney – Old Canal – Cerney Wick

Distance: 5 miles

Map: O.S. Pathfinder 1134, Cricklade

Start: The Crown Inn, Cerney Wick (Grid Reference: SU077959)

Access: The Crown Inn is at the corner of the junction of minor roads in Cerney Wick, between South Cerney and Latton, close to the A419 (Ermin Way) between Cirencester and Swindon. Incredibly, there is a bus stop at the Crown Inn itself, but only for an infrequent bus (no. 63) giving locals the opportunity to shop in Cirencester. It doesn't allow the outsider enough time between buses for a decent walk. This is not a disaster as there is a bus stop on the A419 about half a mile away, where the minor road from Cerney Wick joins it. There are frequent weekday services along this road with buses no 51, X51, X52, and X53 all connecting Cirencester with Swindon. Ask for the stop north of Latton, at the turning to Cerney Wick. The extra mile of road walking (it's a quiet lane) between this bus stop and the pub has been included in the above distance.

The Crown Inn (0793 750369)

The pub has a car park, and it serves real ales, meals and bar snacks. There is a beer garden and a family patio. Opening hours are 12 noon to 3 p.m. and 7 p.m. to 11 p.m. on weekdays, 12 noon to 3 p.m. and 7 p.m. to 10.30 p.m. on Sundays.

The Cotswold Water Park

This is border country, where Gloucestershire meets Wiltshire and the Cotswolds give way to the Thames Valley. Gravel extraction made this a place to avoid for about 60 years. The planners were let loose in the late 1970s, however, to try to make something of it. They designated the large flooded pits as lakes for leisure and wildfowl habitat. Walks and cycleways were marked, utilising the old railway and canal that used to carry passengers and goods through here. The lakes extend for over 1500 acres and are distinguished by the name Cotswold Water park, so a walk around some would seem to be obligatory for a comprehensive exploration of the Cotswolds.

Leaflets about the Water park are available from the Crown Inn, Cerney Wick. They try to sell the area as a holiday resort. Having represented the Swindon Local Group of the Ramblers' Association at the early discussions about this great leisure concept – and knowing the land and dreading the dull hand of bureaucracy – a walk here seemed like deprivation after a series of inspiring rambles along the Cotswold escarpment. But this, too, is the Cotswolds – just about!

The Crown Inn

Having followed this short route, it must be recorded that it made a pleasant, peaceful, experience. Yes, these lakes are artificial, but so are the lakes in the Elan Valley. Bring a camera on a sunny weekend and you'll be able to take pictures of colourful yachts. You could even take out temporary membership of a sailing club, or try windsurfing. Unauthorised swimming is discouraged because of the danger of deep water with hidden obstructions and weed growth. You are invited to learn to water-ski and even hire a jet ski by the half hour. Holiday accommodation, including 300 pitches for touring caravans and camping is available. There is a Round House on the Thames and Severn Canal near Cerney Wick. The disused railway line is the Midland and South Western Junction Railway, which ran between Andover and Cheltenham via Swindon.

The wildfowl on the lakes includes grebes, herons, Canadian geese, mute swans, and pochard.

The Walk

Go over the stile behind the road signpost at the T-junction opposite the Crown Inn. Cross a field to pass a tree nursery on your left and take the stile beside a signpost in the hedge ahead. Continue over a lane and the stile on the far side.

Pass a house and a garden wall on your right. Go over a stile in the next corner and follow the fence on your right for 20 yards. Cross the stile ahead and walk with the fence, which soon becomes a hedge, on your left. Pass Lake no 9 (used by the Cotswold Sailing Club) on your right. Follow the path as it turns right in a corner ahead. Keep beside the hedge on your left as you turn left at the next corner, with the lake still on your right.

Look for a waymark post with a yellow arrow and a white dot (no, it's not for the Cotswold Way) at the next corner. Go left down steps, then cross a footbridge. Follow a hedge, which becomes a fence, on your left. Go over a stile near a signpost in the next corner and set foot on the disused railway.

Turn right to walk along the disused railway towards South Cerney. Ignore a signposted path over a footbridge on your left, then pass a stile

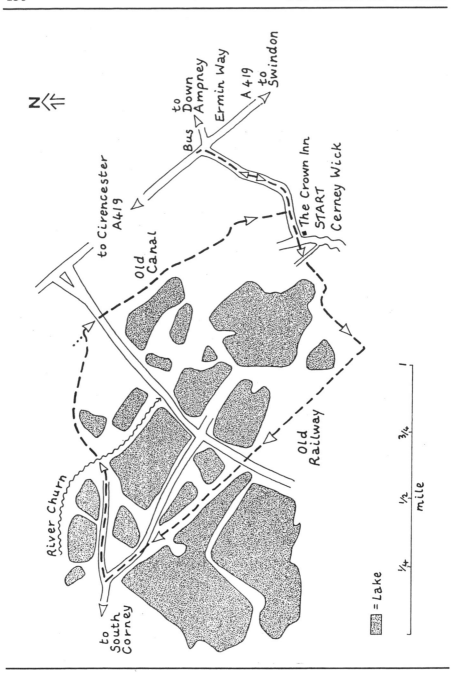

N

to
Down
Ampney
Bus

Ermin Way

A 4-19

to
Swindon

to Cirencester
A419

The Crown Inn
START
Cerney Wick

Old
Canal

Old
Railway

River Churn

to
South
Corney

= Lake

¼   ½   ¾
          mile

on your right. Continue past a footbridge on your right, go ahead carefully across a road and follow the old railway between lakes.

Reach another road and go left, as waymarked, along a wide, grassy verge. Look for a signpost with a red dot on it and turn right along Wilmoorway Lane. Go over a bridge across the old railway and follow the lane between lakes.

Bear right over a stile beside a signpost bearing a red dot and showing that Cerney Wick is $1^1/_2$ miles away. Walk with a lake on your right and parallel to the lane on your left. Cross a stile in the next corner and go ahead to a signpost above a footbridge.

Take the footbridge, which is to the right of a bridge carrying the lane, over the River Churn. Walk along the track ahead and cross a waymarked stile to the right of a gate. A wonderfully secluded path leads to the disused Thames and Severn Canal.

Turn right over a stile and follow the towpath of the old canal, as signposted to Cerney Wick (one mile). You soon cross a road and continue, as signposted, on the other side. Ignore a footbridge and a signposted path to the River Churn on your right. Go ahead to the Cerney Wick road, near an old lock and the Round House.

Turn right along the road for the Crown Inn at the junction in Cerney Wick. If your imperative is the bus which passes along the A419, however, turn left to follow this quiet road to its junction with the main road, on the old Roman Ermin Way. The bus stop is on your left.

22. WOTTON-UNDER-EDGE

Route: Wotton-under-Edge – Brackenbury Ditches – Tyndale Monument – The New Inn – Wotton-under-Edge

Distance: 6 miles

Map: O.S. Pathfinder 1132 Dursley & Wotton-under-Edge

Start: The Falcon Inn, Wotton-under-Edge (Grid Reference: ST759933)

Access: The Falcon is at 20 Church Street, Wotton-under-Edge. This isn't far from St Mary's Church and the war memorial, where the buses stop. These include the number 10 service from Stroud on weekdays and the 309 between Bristol and Dursley via Wotton-under-Edge and the 626 between Bristol and Dursley via Wotton-under-Edge.

The Falcon Inn (0453 842138)

This 17th century coaching inn has a ghost of an old lady in the attic. New bar staff had just made acquaintance with it when I visited, so she may appear for you if you care to sample the overnight accommodation. There is light music on Thursday evenings, while Tuesday nights are enlivened by quizzes. Real ale, bar meals and snacks are served, while the staff couldn't be friendlier. Opening hours are 12 noon to 3 p.m. and 6 p.m. to 11 p.m. on weekdays, 12 noon to 3 p.m. and 7 p.m. to 10.30 p.m. on Sundays.

The New Inn, North Nibley (0453 3659)

This lively, welcoming but remote pub comes about halfway round this route. It stands in magnificent surroundings and has a large garden with a children's play area. Accommodation and meals are available while the real ales include Cotleigh WB, Tawny Bitter, Greene King Abbot, Smiles Best Bitter and Theakston's Old Peculier. Opening hours are 11 a.m. (12 noon in winter) to 2.30 p.m. and 6 p.m. (7 p.m. in winter) to 11 p.m.

Wotton-under-Edge

Wotton occupies a delightful spot under the edge, or at the foot of the Cotswold escarpment. It was burnt to the ground by King John's mercenaries in the early 13th century because of the town's connection with the Berkeley family of nearby Berkeley Castle. This enabled it to be rebuilt as a planned town which became a borough in 1253. The present church of St Mary the Virgin was consecrated in 1283.

Wool brought prosperity in the 17th and 18th centuries and the Perry Almshouses, in Church Street, near the Falcon Inn, were erected in 1638. Go through the doorway into the courtyard and look back to see, above the passage, a list of regulations for the residents. Also around this courtyard are the Dawes Almshouses and General Hospital which were built in about 1720.

As you start the walk up Long Street, notice Church House on the first corner on your left. This is known to have existed in 1476. The next corner on your left brings Orchard Street. A short diversion up it will show you the house where Isaac Pitman, inventor of the shorthand system, lived. Back on Long Street, the building on your right now occupied by Lloyd's Bank was once an inn from which stage coaches left for Cirencester.The little Tolsey House on the corner of Market Street and High Street served as a market court in the 16th century. Continuing up High Street, the National Westminster Bank building was given its present appearance in Regency times. There is a small museum at Ludgate Hill, adjoining the county library and near the Falcon Inn. This is open on Saturdays (10 a.m. to 12 noon) and on summer Tuesdays (2.30 p.m. to 4.30 p.m.).

Brackenbury Ditches

This Iron Age hillfort is now obscured by trees, but your path passes its two widely spaced eastern banks and ditches, which face a mass of relatively flat land. The other two sides of the triangular promontory only need a single rampart and ditch to cap their steep slopes.

The Tyndale Monument

This 111 ft high tower was erected in 1866 in memory of William Tyndale, the first translator of the New Testament into English.

The Tyndale monument

Reputedly born near this spot (they will tell you differently at Slimbridge), he suffered martyrdom at Vilvorde in Flanders on 6th October 1536. A nearby topograph helps to identify landmarks, such as the Severn Bridge (12 miles away), the Sugar Loaf near Abergavenny in Gwent (33 miles away and 1955 ft high), Haresfield Beacon (10 miles away) and Ozleworth Tower (3 miles away). It is a curious fact that such 19th century monuments do happen to have been built on leys. Perhaps this was by design, perhaps by chance. In this case, a ley can be dowsed going through the entrance of the monument to a tumulus at ST 789964 and on to the church at Avening.

The Walk

With your back to the Falcon Inn, go left and turn right immediately up Long Street. Pass Market Street on your left and continue as High Street to a crossroads. Go ahead up Bradley Street. Bear right with this and turn left at an upper road junction. Pass Old London Road on your right. 50 yards after it, bear right up the waymarked Cotswold Way (notice the white dot with the yellow arrow).

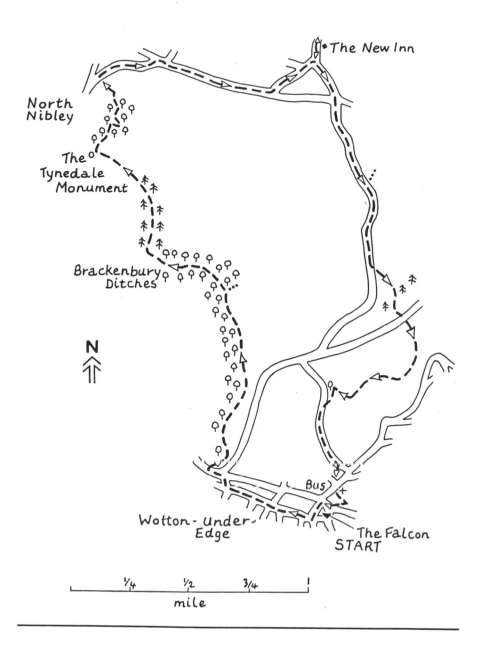

The New Inn

North
Nibley

The
Tynedale
Monument

Brackenbury
Ditches

N

Bus

Wotton-Under-
Edge

The Falcon
START

1/4   1/2   3/4

mile

This steep, handrailed, path bends right to a stile. Cross this to follow the enclosed path. Continue over a lane and up steps to a stile opposite. Bear left to a waymark post and climb Wotton Hill. A plantation of trees was planted to commemorate the Battle of Waterloo, but these were felled by the end of the Crimean War; they were replaced by a plantation behind this walled enclosure in 1887 (Queen Victoria's Jubilee). Extra trees were planted to mark Queen Elizabeth II's accession to the throne in 1952.

Pass the plantation on your left and cross a stile in the fence ahead, at the top of the hill. This is still the Cotswold Way, so look for a white dot with the yellow waymark arrow. Continue along the left-hand edge of a field on this plateau, above the wooded slope on your left. Go through a gap in the corner ahead to follow the blue waymarked bridle way, keeping above Westridge wood on your left and passing a field on your right.

Ignore a track on your right as you enter woodland ahead. Follow the white dots of the Cotswold Way across a forest track, then go right at the next fork. Pass Brackenbury Ditches on your left. Go ahead at the next crosstracks and bear right to keep above the escarpment on your left. Go right at a junction, then turn left to emerge from the wood.

Follow a fence on your left to the Tyndale Monument. Admire the view over the Severn estuary into Wales, with the aid of the topograph placed below the tower to mark the Silver Jubilee of Queen Elizabeth II in 1977.

Go right from the Tyndale Monument, keeping above the trees and the escarpment on your left. Take the waymarked Cotswold Way into the wood but do not turn sharply left down a broad track. Instead, leave the Cotswold Way here by turning right. Take the smaller of two gates ahead, go ahead 10 yards and turn left over a stile to re-enter the wood. Follow the path which descends steeply through the trees on your right, to a stile in the bottom corner. Turn left over it and go down a path to the road which runs from North Nibley to Waterley Bottom.

Go right along the road (away from North Nibley). Keep right at a junction near a telephone box. Go as signposted towards Waterley Bottom. Take the next turning on your left and go ahead up a No Through Road to The New Inn.

Retrace your steps from The New Inn and take the first turning on your left. This leads to a crossroads. Take the lane ahead signposted as '1 in 7 Steep Hill Wotton-under-Edge' (that'll keep the cars away!). Pass Brookside Cottage on your left. Ignore a hedged and signposted path going sharply left. Do take the next path which is signposted on your left. This is a hedged bridleway which gradually climbs to the wood ahead. Continue through the wood, bearing right to the top and ignoring tracks which join your bridleway, waymarked with blue arrows. Continue along a hedged track to the Old London Road.

Go ahead across the road to follow the signposted path opposite. Start between a wall on your left and a barn on your right. When the hedged path bears left downhill, go straight ahead over a waymarked stile in the corner. Walk beside a wall on your right on the top of Coombe Hill (Coombe is the same as the Welsh cwm, or valley).

Continue around a bend with a fence on your right, go right at the next corner and cross a stile beside a gate. Take the fenced path ahead. Turn sharply left along the descending path which is waymarked by a yellow arrow and runs beside a fence on your left. Soon fork right to go between the trees and down steps to a stile above a house. Continue to descend to a road.

Go left along the road, looking for a 'No Cycling' sign on your right. Bear right along this estate path, with a wall on your left and the tower of St Mary's Church ahead. Cross the road to enter the churchyard and leave it by the iron gates opposite the porch of the church. Take the waymarked path (with the white dot of the Cotswold Way again) and go right to reach the war memorial and the bus stops. Church Street, with the Falcon Inn near its end, is on your left.

23. SOUTH OF TETBURY

Route: The Crown Inn, Tetbury – Estcourt House – Shipton Moyne – Westonbirt – Highgrove House – The Crown Inn, Tetbury

Distance: 8^1/$_2$ miles

Maps: O.S. Pathfinders 1133 Nailsworth and 1152 Malmesbury

Start: The Crown Inn, Tetbury (Grid Reference: ST892932)

Access: The Crown Inn is near the top of Gumstool Hill, where it joins the B4014 (Silver Street) in the centre of Tetbury. The A4135 from Dursley meets the A433 from Cirencester at Tetbury, where there is car parking, including in front of the Crown Inn. Buses stop around the corner in Long Street. The no. 31 is a good weekday service from Stroud (some buses from Gloucester), while there is also a weekday no. 28 service from Stroud. Bus no. X46 runs from Stroud on Tuesdays only, while Alex Cars provide a service between Tetbury and Kemble railway station on weekdays. (tel. Cirencester 653985).

The Crown Inn (0666 502469)

This substantial building dates back to 1693 and is reputedly the home of a ghost. Flowers Real Ale is for sale, and there is food and accommodation on the premises. Monday to Friday opening hours are 11 a.m. to 2.30 p.m. and 5.30 p.m. to 11 p.m. On Saturdays they are 11 a.m. to 2.30 p.m. and 6.30 p.m. to 11 p.m. Sunday opening hours are noon to 2.30 p.m. and 7 p.m. to 10.30 p.m.

Tetbury

This attractive market town is now famous as the place where Princess Diana and sometimes Princess Anne shop. Here are the royal baker and greengrocer – look out for the Prince of Wales' feathers adorning these shops! All the warrant holders are invited to a Christmas party and a summer garden party at Highgrove. Perhaps Princess Eugenie was to receive the Jemima Puddleduck bubble bath which Princess Diana was spotted buying before Christmas 1991 at Norman Bell, the chemists in Church Street. Its price was £3.19. Princess Beatrice went with her aunt to choose her own present of a doll's china tea-set, costing £5.99 at Poppets. Diana also bought £25 of white stretch suits here for her friends' babies. If you spend awhile browsing in the Tolsey bookshop, you'll be following a royal example, while the Princes William and Harry have their riding gear bought from the Tack Shop. The florist shop, Coates, provides Wills and Harry with their favourite glittery helium balloons at £1.99 each. The Waleses also order their favourite blue, yellow and white flowers for the house from here.

Tetbury has a long history, with a record of a Saxon monastery here in 681. St Mary's church has a striking 186 ft high tower. This is a replica of the medieval tower and spire which were taken down in 1891. The rest of the building had been rebuilt between 1777 and 1781 under the direction of the architect Francis Hiorn. An early example of a Gothic revival church, it has high box pews, very large windows and a passage around its interior, which is like a church within a church. There is an air of grace and elegance, making a visit well worthwhile.

Tetbury Market

The Market House dates from 1655 and is supported on stout stone pillars. The Snooty Fox Hotel nearby used to boast a large ballroom on its first floor for the famous Beaufort Hunt to get up to their jolly japes. It is now divided into bedrooms. Wool brought prosperity to the town and it is heavy (65lb) sacks of wool that have to be carried up and down the 1 in 4 gradient of Gumstool Hill on Woolsack Day (Spring Bank Holiday Monday). Stall-holders turn out in medieval dress, while there is a town jester and morris dancing.

Shipton Moyne

The church of St John the Baptist was rebuilt by the Victorians, but records go back to Norman times. The architect was T.H.Wyatt, whose relative James Wyatt was the pre-eminent architect of the late 18th century and lies buried in Westminster Abbey. If you are thirsty, the Cat and Custard Pot Inn lies beside your path and serves real ale. If your courage deserts you in this pub, there is a bus stop outside for Tetbury (no. G51). You might have a long wait however, as the service runs on Tuesday and Friday mornings only.

Westonbirt

Westonbirt House is now a girls' school and is not open to the public, although you will follow a right of way through its grounds. Allow plenty of time, if possible, for a diversion to Westonbirt Arboretum. This is one of the finest and largest collections of trees and shrubs in the world and was founded by Robert Stayner Holford of Westonbirt House in 1829. Acquired by the Forestry Commission in 1956, it is managed as an important national tree collection and research establishment. The public is free to wander anywhere and admire the 17,000 trees and shrubs. Several recommended trails are waymarked and it is advisable to purchase trail guidebooks in the visitor centre. A snack bar is open to provide refreshments daily (10 a.m. to 5 p.m.) except in the winter, while the Arboretum is open every day of the year (10 a.m. to 8 p.m. or dusk if earlier). October is the most popular month, but weekends then can get crowded. An admission charge is payable at the entrance.

The Walk

The Crown Inn

With your back to the Crown Inn, bear right to Silver Street. Go left downhill towards Long Newnton and notice an old gas lamp bracket on the side of a house on your left. A plaque records that 'Tetbury was first lit by gas in 1836'. Cross a valley with the elevated road and turn right along a lane which is signposted as a public footpath. Approach a gate across it and veer right to go over a waymarked stile beside a fieldgate. Bear right to walk beside a fence (becoming a wall) on your left to a second stile. Continue beside the wall on your left and over three more stiles in corners ahead.

Cross a track leading away to your left and go over a wooden stile ahead to walk beside a hedge on your right. Continue over a stile in the corner, with the hedge still on your right, to a gate in it. Bear right through this gate.

Cross a stone footbridge, then a wooden footbridge and a subsequent stile. Go straight ahead up a field for a quarter of a mile, to a drive (this is in Estcourt Park). Go right at a fork and follow it for half a mile to pass farm buildings and stables on your left. Emerge over a cattle grid near a house on your right. Bear right across grass as shown by a waymark arrow. Take a gate in a hedge and cross three fields as waymarked with arrows on wooden stiles to reach another drive.

Go left along the drive and pass an access lane to a farm on your left. Approach Hodges Farmhouse (ahead) and turn right through a gate near it (and not the waymarked kissing-gate before it). Cross a field to a stile and continue through a kissing-gate into the churchyard at St John's at Shipton Moyne.

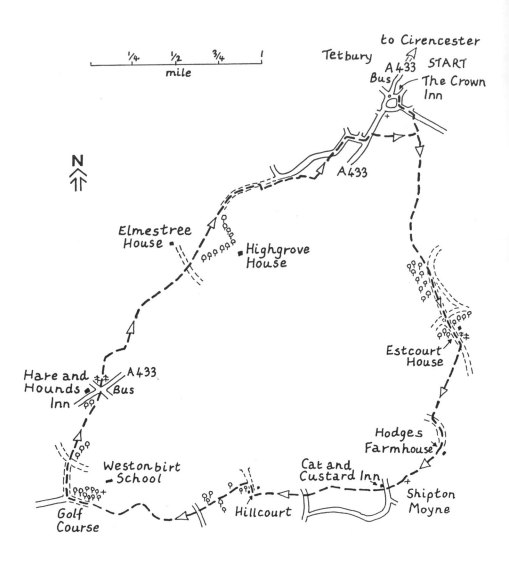

to Cirencester

Tetbury

A433   START

Bus   The Crown
Inn

A433

N

Elmestree
House   ∎Highgrove
         House

Estcourt
House

Hare and   A433
Hounds ∎   Bus
Inn

Hodges
Farmhouse

Cat and
Custard Inn

Westonbirt
∎ School

Shipton
Moyne

Golf   Hillcourt
Course

Proceed to the road through the village and cross it carefully to the Cat and Custard Pot Inn opposite. Take the footpath signposted ahead to pass this pub on your right. A wooden step stile leads into a field. Go ahead to cross two more wooden step stiles and reach a stone stile. This leads to a paddock which is left by another wooden stile ahead.

Walk with a wall on your right to reach a corner with a double stile to cross before reaching a road at a signpost. Go right for 10 yards then turn left over a signposted stile to walk with a fence on your left. Go slightly right to a waymarked gate in the wall ahead. Pass through it and cross a paddock to a waymarked gate in the next wall.

Maintain your direction across the next field to a gate in the far right corner. Go through it and turn left to follow yellow arrows through the farmyard at Hillcourt. Walk right along the farm's access track but turn left, as waymarked, at the end of the farm buildings. Go through a gate and follow the hedge on your left to another gate. Continue with a fence on your left through a gate ahead. Veer slightly right across the next field to a gate giving access to a road.

Cross the road to a gate opposite and follow the signposted path across parkland. Take a gate in the fence ahead and notice Westonbirt School to the right. Continue through a small, wooden gate on your right and turn left to follow a wall on your left to a pond. Veer right to cross a stile onto a golf course. Follow its access drive (with a wall on your right) to a road.

Turn right up the private drive of Westonbirt School (this is a public path). At a T-junction, with the school on your right and the drive to Westonbirt Arboretum on your left, take the grassy path ahead across parkland. Go through a kissing-gate beside a fieldgate in the fence ahead. Keep just to the right of a wood ahead to pass the Hare and Hounds Hotel on the other side of the road on your left. Leave the park through the iron kissing-gate in the far corner.

Cross the busy crossroads (A433) with care. The Hare and Hounds Hotel is behind you on the left and the bus shelter for the X46 to Tetbury and Stroud (Tuesday afternoons only) is on your right. Take the small gate beside the signpost ahead. Pass through a belt of conifer trees to a small gate giving access to a field.

Go ahead to a stile to the left of a gate in the fence opposite. Continue to a hedge and turn right to walk with it on your left. Pass a gate on your left and turn left over a stile just after it. Cut across a field to the stone stile in the hedge opposite. Maintain this direction to the far corner of the next field.

Cross a stone stile and go right along a track which has a wooden fence on your left and a hedge on your right. Continue over a stone stile in the next corner and cross pasture to a wooden stile in the fence ahead. Go ahead over parkland and a drive to reach a waymarked gate to the left of a pond. Go through a second waymarked gate to the next field. Highgrove House, the home of the Prince Charles and Princess Diana is about 400 yards away to your right, behind a screen of trees.

Walk with a fence on your left and go slightly right to the waymarked gate in the fence ahead. Maintain this direction across the next field to a waymarked gate in the corner. Pass Elmestree Lodge on your left and follow its access lane. Ignore a signposted path on your left but do cross a stone stile on your right soon after it.

Turn left immediately to follow a path parallel to the narrow lane on your left. Cross a stone stile in the corner, go ahead over a track and continue across a waymarked wooden stile. Keep walking parallel to the lane on your left.

Head slightly right to a stone stile in a wall ahead. Turn left over a subsequent footbridge and turn right through trees to follow a wall on your left. Fork left to a stile at the end of this plantation. Cross into a field and go straight ahead to a stone stile beside a signpost which stands to the left of a bungalow in the far right corner.

Turn right along the pavement of Longfurlong Lane. Go right at a junction (Berrells Road) and reach the A433. Go left towards Tetbury. Look for a bus stop on the far side of this road (for buses leaving Tetbury) and go across the road carefully to turn right just before it.

Cross a stile beside a gate near a signpost. Veer left immediately through a waymarked metal kissing-gate. Follow the path past the earthworks of an old ring and bailey below St Mary's church on your left. Follow a wall on your left to take a metal kissing-gate which is only yards to the left of the stile crossed on your outward journey. Retrace your steps to the Crown Inn.

24. HAWKESBURY UPTON

Route: Hawkesbury Upton – Horton Court – Cotswold Way – Somerset Monument – Hawkesbury Upton

Distance: 5 miles

Map: O.S. Pathfinder 1151 Patchway & Chipping Sodbury

Start: The Duke of Beaufort Inn (Grid Reference: ST 777870)

Access: There is a car park at this pub in the village which is just off the A46, between Bath and Nailsworth. The most useful bus service to Hawkesbury Upton is likely to be no 623 run by Fosseway between Bristol and Wotton-under-Edge. Telephone 0249 782401. Badgerline (tel. 0272 297979) run service numbers X69 and 342 from Bristol but these will get you to the village in the evening and take you away from it in the morning.

The Duke of Beaufort Inn (0454 23217)

Fullers London Pride and Exmoor Gold are among the real ales served here. Food is available, while there is a resident ghost notorious for turning the gas off in the cellar. Originally an early 18th century farmhouse (on the Beaufort estate), the property has its own 50 ft well. Opening hours are 11.30 a.m. to 2 p.m. and 7 p.m. to 11 p.m. on Mondays; 12 noon to 2 p.m. and 7 p.m. to 11 p.m. on Tuesdays; 6.30 p.m. to 11 p.m. (evenings only) on Wednesdays; 12 noon to 2 p.m. and 6.30 p.m. to 11 p.m. on Thursdays; 12 noon to 2 p.m. and 6.30 p.m. to 11 p.m. on Fridays; 12 noon to 3 p.m. and 7 p.m. to 11 p.m. on Saturdays; and 12 noon to 2 p.m. and 7 p.m. to 10.30 p.m. on Sundays.

Horton Court

Dr William Knight, who negotiated with the Vatican on Henry VIII's behalf for a divorce from Catherine of Aragon, had the Court and ambulatory built in the 16th century. A Norman hall dating back to the

12th century stands within the grounds, while the Church of St James the Elder is adjacent. Managed by the National Trust, the Court is open to the public on Wednesdays and Saturdays from April to October, between 2 p.m. and 6 p.m.

The Somerset Monument

The Somerset Monument

This exotic tower, with an Indian style that is not justified by any connection of Lord Somerset with India, was designed by the architect Lewis Vulliamy in 1846.

It is a memorial to Lord Edward Somerset, of the Beaufort family, who fought at Waterloo and lived to the age of 66, dying in 1842. A magnificent viewpoint and landmark, it is possible to climb its 144 steps and brave the wind to see across the Forest of Dean into Wales.

Hawkesbury Upton

The village used to be clustered around the old Saxon church of St Mary's at the foot of the hill. Its migration to the top is said to have been a response to a tragedy. The lord of the manor's daughter fell out of the window to her death while waving farewell to her lover. The old manor house, down by the church, was allowed to go to rack and ruin and has vanished. The village's name may be derived from Havoche's hill or camp.

The Duke of Beaufort

The Walk

Face the Duke of Beaufort Inn and take the path ahead on the left, signposted to Norton. Bear right off the surfaced path after 50 yards to go over the grass to a stile in the hedge on your right. Cross the stile and turn half left over a field to a stile in the hedge opposite.

Go ahead to join a hedge on your right and take the gap in the hedge that comes to join in at a right angle from the left. Keeping the hedge on your right, go ahead to a track (Bath Lane, part of the Cotswold Way, along which you will return) and go left a few yards until there is a gate on your right.

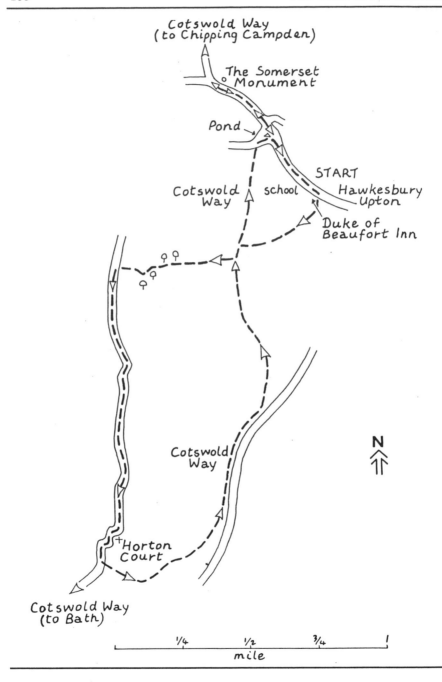

Cotswold Way
(to Chipping Campden)

The Somerset
Monument

Pond

Cotswold
Way

school

START
Hawkesbury
Upton

Duke of
Beaufort Inn

Cotswold
Way

N

Horton
Court

Cotswold Way
(to Bath)

¼   ½   ¾   1
mile

Turn right through the gate and go ahead along a track with a hedge oh your right. Continue through a gate and descend beside a fence on your right to another gate. Go ahead along an old green lane which bends right. Cross a stile beside a gate next to a signpost at its end to emerge on a minor road.

Turn left along the road and reach Horton Court, on your left. Continue past the Church of St James the Elder and come to a Cotswold Way signpost next to a stile beside a gate on your left. Turn left over the stile to follow the Cotswold Way.

Go ahead past a hedge on your left and up a field to a waymarked stile beside a gate. Continue through woodland up to a waymark post. Turn left up steps and walk along a path at the top of the woodland and near a fence on your right. Turn right over a waymarked stile in this fence, then bear left to follow the well-trodden and waymarked path which climbs to take a waymarked gap in a hedge ahead.

Pass a building which has lost its roof on your right and cross a stile in the far right corner ahead. Continue with a lane on your right, walking along the edge of the field. Follow the Cotswold Way's distinctive yellow arrows with white dots to a stile in the hedge ahead This is to the left of a building. Cross the stile and resume walking with a hedge, on your right and parallel to the lane.

When the hedge bears left, away from the lane, go through a waymarked gap on your right and turn left immediately to follow the hedge on your left. Keep to this waymarked track (Bath Lane) all the way to the road at Home Farm.

Turn right to pass the pond and reach a T-junction Divert left along the road for nearly half a mile to see the Somerset Monument, on your right. Return to pass the pond on your right and go ahead along the road into Hawkesbury Upton. Follow the pavement to pass the school on your right, then come to the Duke of Beaufort, on your right.

25. OLD SODBURY

Route: Chipping Sodbury – Portway Lane – Little Sodbury – St Adeline's Church – Sodbury Hillfort – Cotswold Way – Old Sodbury – Frome Valley Walkway – Chipping Sodbury

Distance: 5¹/₂ miles

Path: O.S. Pathfinder 1151 Patchway & Chipping Sodbury

Start: The Boot Inn (Grid Reference: ST 732821)

Access: There is a good bus service right to the door of this pub. Take Badgerline's services nos 340, 341, 342, 628 and 629 from Bristol (tel. 0272 297979). The Boot is in Horse Street, Chipping Sodbury, and has its own car park for patrons.

The Boot Inn (0454 312098)

'Bob', a local real ale called Broad Oak Bitter and brewed in Wickwar, is served here, as is good food (with vegetarians catered for). Originally a late 17th century farmhouse, there has long been a pub here. Animals used to be kept in a pound next door, before their sale in Chipping Sodbury market – hence the saying that you could 'buy beer by the pound at the Boot'. The great early 20th century all round athlete C.B. Fry used to drink here and the locals will be pleased to tell you all about his many achievements. Opening hours are 11 a.m. to 2.30 p.m. and 7 p.m. to 11 p.m. on weekdays, 12 noon to 2.30 p.m. and 7 p.m. to 10.30 p.m. on Sundays.

THE SODBURYS

Chipping Sodbury is the most recent settlement with the Sodbury place-name. Sod may refer to the Celtic God Sul (as in Silbury Hill) while bury means a fort or camp. This is an ancient site, as witnessed by the Iron Age hillfort. Rectangular in shape, this covers an area of about 12 acres. The double ramparts are widely spaced, being about 100 ft apart. The Romans found this made a useful frontier post when they invaded Britain and the hillfort is known locally as Roman Camps. The Saxon army also stayed here in 577 before the Battle of Durham (see Walk 26). There is even more history under this turf, with Edward IV's army resting here on their way to fight Margaret of Anjou's supporters at the Battle of Tewkesbury in 1471. Little Sodbury is where St Adeline's Church stands. The dedication is to the patron saint of Flemish weavers. It was built in 1859 from the stones and plan of William Tyndale's little chapel behind Little Sodbury Manor. Tyndale lived here during Henry VIII's reign and felt here the call to see that before he died 'every ploughboy in England shall read the Bible as easily as the pope in Rome'.

St Adeline's church, Little Sodbury

Both the Cotswold Way and the Bristol Countryway follow this route from Little Sodbury to Old Sodbury, over the hillfort.

Although the 'baby' of the Sodburys, Chipping (which means market) was established by the reign of King Henry III.

The Kingfisher waymarks of the Frome Valley Walkway lead you back to Chipping Sodbury. This route links the Cotswold way with the outskirts of Bristol. Details of it are obtainable for a large s.a.e. from Northavon District Council, Planning Dept, Council Offices, Castle Street, Northbury, Bristol, BS12 1HF.

The Boot

The Walk

Face the Boot and take the path with the 'No Cycling' sign on its right, to pass the pub on your left. Turn left along Gorlands Road, soon passing Melbourne Drive on your left. When Gorlands Road bears right at a triangle, follow its pavement for 100 yards then turn right along the signposted Frome Valley Walk, with a kingfisher waymark.

Walk with the River Frome on your left and past the backs of houses on your right. Go ahead across St John's Way and bear right over grass to an iron footbridge. Use it to cross the River Frome and continue over a

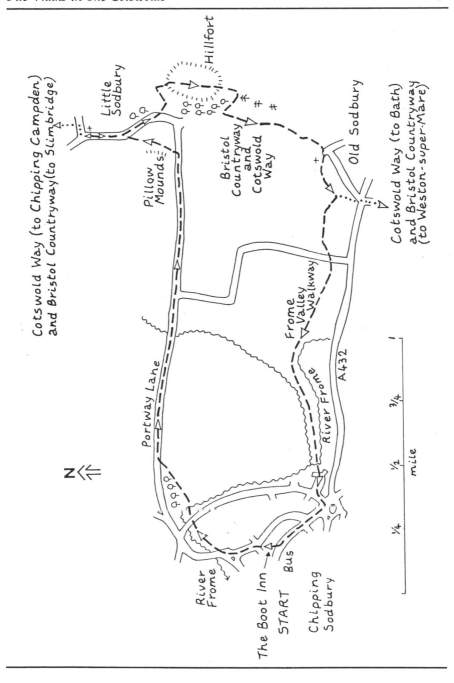

corner of a field to cross a second, wooden, footbridge. Go ahead over the subsequent stile and up a long field with woodland on your left.

Continue over a stile beside a signpost in the hedge ahead. Reach Portway Lane and turn right to walk over the open common alongside it. Pass Harwoodgate Farm on your right and continue along a hedged lane for one mile until there is a stile in the hedge on your left.

Turn left over the stile and go ahead over old pillow mounds to reach a gate to the right of a house ahead. Go through this to a lane and turn left along it to visit St Adeline's Church, Little Sodbury, on your right. Retrace your steps and climb with the lane up to a Cotswold Way signpost on your left.

Turn left, then right along the waymarked Cotswold Way. Walk with a hedge on your right to a gate in the corner. Go through this and turn left, as waymarked, to climb past tree-clad earthworks to buildings. Turn right, as waymarked, to pass the first building on your left.

Turn left over a stile in a fence on your left and follow the waymarked route which goes ahead before turning right to cross the hillfort. Reach a stile in a wall (to the right of a gate) on the far side. Cross this and turn right down an enclosed path. Use the stone steps to the left of a gate to cross a stile and continue descending with a fence on your left.

Reach a Cotswold Way waymark post and turn sharply left over the stile above a gate. Follow the path ahead which keeps above the fence and hedge on your right. Eventually cross a stile beside a small wooden gate in the far corner. Take the track ahead, with a wall on your left and a hedge on your right.

Pass a school on your left and bear right to the churchyard of St John the Baptist's, Old Sodbury. Pass this church on your right to follow the waymarked Cotswold Way through a kissing gate out of the churchyard. Bear slightly left downhill to a stile in the bottom left corner. Cross this and bear right, as waymarked, over the next field to a stile beside a gate in the hedge opposite. Don't go over this! Depart from the Cotswold Way here by turning sharply right to re-cross the field diagonally to a stile in the far corner.

Cross the stile and veer left to continue over a stile in the middle of the opposite hedge. Bear left, as waymarked, after crossing this to go over a stile in the next hedge and reach a road. Take the stile on the far side of the road to follow the signposted Frome Valley Walkway, with its kingfisher waymarks.

Veer very slightly left over the field to a stile in the hedge opposite Continue over the next field to a stile and keep to the well-trodden path across the following field to join a stream on your left and eventually reach a stile in a hedge ahead.

Go ahead up a long meadow, ignore a bridge on your left but cross a stile in the fence ahead. Follow the path up the next long meadow to a footbridge in its far right corner. Cross this to go right with the signposted Frome Valley Walkway.

Take the first path on your left to reach a road. Go ahead up Wickham Close to St John's Way. Go left to a roundabout and turn right along Horse Street to return to The Boot, on your right.

26. DYRHAM

Route: Tolldown – Bristol Countryway – West Littleton – Dyrham – Cotswold Way – Tolldown

Distance: 5 miles

Map: O.S. Pathfinder 1167 Bristol (East)

Start: The Crown Inn, Tolldown (Grid Reference: ST 754769)

Access: Motorists should start at the Tolldown Inn, which stands beside the A46 just south of the M4 Tormarton Interchange 18. There is a car park for patrons. It's more fun to come by bus, however. In this case, start halfway round at Dyrham and walk an extra quarter of a mile each way (this is included in the walk total of five miles) from the bus stop at Dyrham Home Farm. The bus service is provided by a cheerful independent operator who deserves your support. This is the infrequent 620 service operated by Crown Coaches (tel. 0272 710251) between Bath and Chipping Sodbury, whose timetable should allow this walk to be enjoyed on a Wednesday or a Saturday.

The Crown Inn, Tolldown (0225 891231)

The ghost of an old lady in a red dress of the late 18th century, when nearby Bath was the fashionable resort, has been seen by guests staying here, so why not try bed and breakfast? The real ale is exciting too, including Wadworth's 6X, Old Timer and Tanglefoot, a guest bitter which is deceptively easy to drink but is really strong. Perhaps it was around in the mid 19th century when a pub brawl led to a man being killed here. He might be the ghost that knocks glasses off their hooks and throws ashtrays from the bar. Meals and snacks are available in this old coaching inn, dating from at least 1700, when it was on the road between Bristol and London. Vegetarians are catered for and there is a garden for children to play in. Opening hours are 11 a.m. to 2.30 p.m. and 6 p.m. to 11 p.m. from Mondays to Fridays, 11 a.m. to 2.30 p.m. and 7 p.m. to 11 p.m. on Saturdays, with 12 noon to 2.30 p.m. and 7 p.m. to 10.30 p.m. on Sundays.

The Crown Inn

DYRHAM

It could be said that England was born here in the blood and turmoil of battle. A most decisive victory by the Saxons over the Britons was he Battle of Dyrham in 577. The Saxon chieftains Caewlin and Cuthvine of Wessex broke through the British territory at a strategic spot, leading to the isolation of the Cornish from their compatriots in Wales.

From now on the Saxons held the upper hand, and contained the British in the Celtic fringe and imposed their own language and culture over what was to become known as England. Three British leaders were slain here, Commail, Condidan and Farinmail.Their defeat delivered the cities of Bath, Cirencester and Gloucester to the Saxons. It was also a reversal of fortunes for the British, after the golden era of King Arthur. The Anglo-Saxon Chronicle records the date of this battle as 577 AD, while Welsh Annals give Arthur's last battle (in the civil war with his nephew Mordred, at Camlan) as about 540 'in the year of Our Lord'. Now the Britons may well have counted the Incarnation of Our Lord as being his baptism by John, or even his crucifixion in the Gnostic manner. The Celtic Church stemmed from Joseph of Arimathea's arrival with the holy

Grail at Glastonbury, centuries before St Augustine's mission from Rome to Kent. This means that King Arthur's death or legendary disappearance could have preceded the Battle of Dyrham by only a few years, which would be consistent with the effect of the great hero's loss and a destructive civil war on the Britons.

The Battlefield, Dyrham

The Britons lost their supremacy in this island because of their trait of quarrelling between themselves. Encouraged by the weakness of the Britons, the Saxons drove home their advantage, leaving the Britons to languish in the hell of enslavement able only to await the day when the light of liberation would shine on them again. It is said that the Saxons were encamped in the old hillfort on Hinton Hill.

The strip lynchets on its slopes, which can be seen from this walk, are probably medieval cultivation terraces Dyrham (pronounced like Durham) means deer enclosure and deer can still be seen in Dyrham Park. William Blathwayt, the Secretary of State under William III, had the house rebuilt as a magnificent mansion in the late 17th century. Set at the foot of 264 acres of parkland, it is now in the care of the National

Trust. The park is open all year, while the house and garden are open from April to October from Saturday to Wednesday inclusive, between 12 noon and 5.30 p.m.

The Bristol Countryway

A short section of this 81 mile walking route around Bristol is followed to West Littleton. Starting at Slimbridge and reaching the sea at Weston-super-Mare, the Countryway visits Berkeley Castle, Bath Abbey, Stanton Drew Stone Circles and Cheddar Gorge. Yours truly's guidebook to the route is published by Thornhill Press of Cheltenham.

The Walk

Go left along the verge of the A46 towards Bath. Bear left through the first gate after the pub garden, and cross the field diagonally to a gate in the far right corner formed by two walls. Maintain your direction across the next field and cross an old stone stile in the wall ahead, on the right in the corner.

Cut across the next field to the corner of the hedge opposite. Go ahead with the hedge on your right and continue through a gap in the next corner. Maintain your direction across the next field to the corner of a hedge and continue with this hedge on your right down to a road (Dunsdown Lane).

Turn left along the lane. When you pass a signposted bridleway on your left you will know that you are now walking a little bit of the route of the Bristol countryway. This follows the lane to West Littleton. Leave it to go south from here while you turn west by taking the signposted path on your right opposite the telephone box.

Pass St James' Church on your right and take the stone stile in the corner of the churchyard wall ahead. Walk past trees on your left and with a fence on your right to a small wooden gate. Veer right, as waymarked, to a fieldgate opposite, marking the end of a wall on the left ahead and with a fence on the right.

Go ahead beside another wall on your right for 20 yards, ignore a waymarked hunting gate on your left but go ahead over the ladder stile in the corner. Descend beside a hedge on your left. Continue over a track to enter the next field.

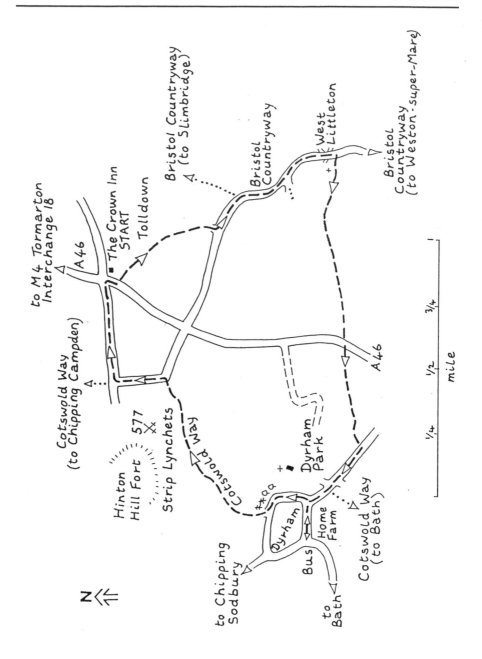

Veer very slightly left to follow the well-trodden path over a drainage ditch and on to a stone stile in the opposite hedge, near where it bends away from you. Cross to the right of this bend and walk with a hedge on your left in the next field.

Veer away slightly to the right of the hedge to reach a gap in the hedge facing you. Continue over the next field and arrive at the A46 beside a roadside signpost. Cross the road very carefully to take the steps up to a squeeze stile in the wall opposite.

Go ahead over a wooden step stile and along a fenced path to, a small wooden gate. Continue beside a high deer fence on your right. Go ahead over a stile in the next corner. Keep beside the deer fence on your right. Continue through a small wooden gate and bear left through newly-planted trees to a stile in the wall which gives access to a road.

Turn right along the road and pass a private road to Sands Farm on your left and a road with a sign stating 'No Entry to Durham Park' on your right (the entrance to the house and park is on the A46).

Enter Dyrham with the Cotswold Way, which has come up from Bath on your left. Reach a grassy triangle with a signpost on it. The way ahead is the walled lane followed by the north-bound Cotswold Way. If you arrive here by bus, however this is where you join and leave the circuit.

Bus passengers simply go down the lane on your left to the bus stop at the next junction. Continuing this route back to the Crown Inn at Tolldown, follow the lane past Dyrham Park on your right. Pass the path giving access to St Peter's Church but take the next turning on your right. This is a rough track with a Cotswold Way signpost.

Climb past trees to a waymarked gate ahead. Go through this to follow a track with a wall on your right. Follow this track through a series of gates to a lane, but look about you on your left. The medieval (or Saxon?) strip lynchets can be made out on the opposite side of the valley, below the hillfort on Hinton Hill. This is the probable ground where the battle was fought and this island's destiny decided in 577.

Turn left along the lane, as signposted for the Cotswold Way. Leave the Way at the T-junction, however, to turn right and walk along the grassy verge to the A46. Cross this busy road carefully and reach the Crown Inn, Tolldown.

27. BATH

Route: Bath – Bus trip to Lansdown Lane – Broadmoor Lane – Cotswold Way – Kelston Round Hill – Weston – Primrose Hill – Royal Avenue – Bath Abbey

Distance: 6 miles plus bus trip

Map: O.S. Pathfinder 1183 Bath & Keynsham

Start: Crystal Palace Inn, G.R. ST 751646; Lansdown Lane Bus Stop, G.R. ST 726670

Access: Normally it is difficult to persuade motorists to use public transport. The convenience of the private car soon snares its owner. There's nothing more inconvenient than a parked car at the wrong end of a linear walk, however. This is why all the other walks in this book are circular. The motorist is thereby denied the prospect of a journey from A to B.

A day's linear walk can cover a surprising variety of country and give that special sense of achievement that comes from reaching a new destination. This thrill at every new dawn is, of course, at the heart of walking long distance paths or trails, especially as a backpacker (a term that can include people who stay in pubs as well as campers) walking the Way in successive days.

The old idea af a pilgrimage soon returns to nourish the soul. For my money, the best long distance walking route in England is the Cotswold Way. Walking it in 1975, I well remember the final stage into Bath, with the tunes of glory in my head sounding like a military band accompanying Lawrence of Arabia into Damascus. Descending upon the city streets like some wild predator from the North (I'd just walked 100 miles from Chipping Campden), the strange noises and surroundings were shut out as I floated along in my private world of exhilarating joy.

Now this book is not a guide to the Cotswold Way. It does take you along well over 100 miles of the Cotswolds, however, including sections of the Cotswold Way. Keep this walk to the last, therefore, as a suitable finale. Having gained a taste for walking in the Cotswolds, do go ahead and backpack the whole of the Cotswold Way.

As I've pointed out in the Introduction, it makes more sense to walk up the map towards Chipping Campden, so you won't have the finish of the real thing debased now. Having recognised the convenience of walking northwards, St James' Church in Chipping Campden is no substitute for Bath Abbey. It is fitting that you give thanks here for a safe journey. Being a city, Bath also has excellent bus services, even on Sundays, to its outskirts. Therefore, walk the few yards from the Crystal Palace Inn (no 10 Abbey Green) to Bath bus station. Go to stop Be in Manvers Street and take bus numbers 14, 14A or 14B (also number 17 from stop Bh in Dorchester Street) to Lansdown Lane, near its corner with Eastfield Avenue.

The Crystal Palace Inn (0225 423944)

You couldn't find a better place to celebrate the end of a long walk. Happily, it's close to Bath Abbey, the bus station and the railway station. There are signposted car parks nearby, while the Tourist Information Centre is around the corner at The Colonnades, Bath Street (tel. 0225 462831). What's more, when I contacted the landlord in the spring of 1992, he was just about to set off on a backpacking trip along the whole of the Cotswold Way!

The Crystal Palace name was adopted after the Great Exhibition in 1851. There has been a pub here since at last 1615 and its previous name was the Three Tuns. Nelson stayed here before leaving to fight the Battle of the Nile (I can't tell you if Lady Hamilton shared his bed), while there is a re-covered Roman mosaic in the cellar. This Georgian open coal fire is still ablaze of a winter's evening, while there are grape vines. With a heated patio and a beer garden, children are a speciality, as are vegetarians. The menu reflects the high reputation of food in Bath. One of the real ales available is Eldridge Pope from an independent Dorchester brewery. Opening Hours are 11 a.m. to 3 p.m. and 6 p.m. to 11 p.m. from Mondays to Fridays, 11 a.m. to 11 p.m. Saturdays and 12 noon to 3 p.m. and 7 p.m. to 10.30 p.m. Sundays.

BATH

There are two legends explaining the discovery of the hot springs that
gave Bath its name and fame. According to Geoffrey of Monmouth, the
ancient British king Bladud (father of Lear) was a shaman or sorcerer. He
attempted to fly with a pair of wings, like Daedalus. He fell and was
dashed to pieces, but not before spotting the magic springs. The more
favoured tale is that the young Bladud suffered from leprosy. An
outcast, he worked as a swineherd. This caused him to notice that the
skins, of the pigs were healed from some ailment when they rooted in a
certain muddy spot. He discovered that the water was warm, even in

Bath Abbey

winter, and that it
cured his leprosy. As
a result, Bladud
succeeded to the
throne and made the
hot springs a sacred
place of healing. The
Romans took to the
idea and built the
famous baths. They
also built a temple
dedicated to Sulis-
Minerva. Minerva was
a Roman goddess and
Sulis is presumed to
be her Celtic equiva-
lent. Some are surpr-
ised at this connec-
tion, having thought
of Sul, Sol or Sil (as at
Silbury Hill) as a sun
god. Feminists have
now promoted the
idea of the sun being
a goddess and the
moon a god, however.
They would, wouldn't
they? Recognising an

unfair contest, I wouldn't dare attempt to disagree. However, the head of Sul in the museum appears masculine to me .

Aquae Sulis was a shadow of its former self when the victorious Saxons arrived after the Battle of Dyrham (see Walk 26) in 577. The first king of all England, Edgar, was crowned here in 973, however. All subsequent coronations have followed the same pattern. The great church belonging to the monastery of St Peter, which the Saxons established, must have been a magnificent building. The Normans replaced it with a vast church whose nave alone is covered by the present abbey. This replaced the almost derelict cathedral church in 1499 and was much restored by Sir Gilbert Scott in the 19th century. The monks had kept the baths going, but medieval Bath was basically a small market town with a reputation for cloth-making, as Chaucer's Wife of Bath shows. The Dissolution led to the baths returning to secular management. When Samuel Pepys visited them in 1668 he remarked that 'it cannot be clean to go so many bodies together in the some water'.

Queen Anne's visit in 1702 made the place fashionable. Richard 'Beau' Nash soon became the flamboyant 'King of Bath', dictating the law even to real royalty. They found obeying the 'King' part of the fun of an extremely well-run 18th century upper-class holiday camp. Graceful buildings were erected, with Royal Crescent (passed on this walk) completed in 1775. The young Horatio Nelson found the young Emma Hamilton, then employed as a servant girl, here. The vices of Bath didn't carry well into Victorian Britain, however. The railway now brought retired colonels and elderly ladies to see out their days in a provincial spa.

The 20th century has brought new visitors, intoxicated by the proximity of so much history. If you see some of them carrying rucksacks, perhaps they've just walked here from Chipping Campden. In March 1992, 1 met some American tourists who had flown over to spend a week's holiday doing exactly that.

A few may even be walking from Land's End to John O'Groats, for Bath is a focal point in the network of long distance paths. The Somerset Way comes up from Minehead (one end of the Sou'West Way from Land's End) to link with the Cotswold Way (which links with other routes to the north to take you to the Pennine Way for Scotland) at Bath Abbey.

The Bristol Countryway also calls here, as does the Bristol to London Walk. The Avon Walkway will also take you to Bristol. There are many attractions to detain backpackers in this city's fleshpots, with a Museum of Costume at the Assembly Rooms, the Roman Baths Museum, Sally Lunn's Kitchen Museum and the American Museum on nearby Claverton Down amongst many others.

The Walk

From the bus stop at the corner of Lansdown Lane with Eastfield Avenue, go left down Lansdown Lane. Turn right up Broadmoor Lane, leading to Broadmoor Vale. Pass Weston All Saints School on your left. Pass an old City of Bath/Somerset boundary post at the end of a housing estate on your right.

Continue past the access lane to Aldermead on your right, then bear right at a fork. Go left at the next fork to follow a muddy, hedged track. Continue through a small gate beside a fieldgate waymarked with a white arrow. Take the wide track which veers left to run with a hedge on your left and a fence on your right.

Go through a gate into a belt of woodland and bear left up a sunken track. Bear right to a gate in the top fence and go left up a hedged track to join the Cotswold Way at a signpost. Turn left over a stile beside a small metal gate to follow the Cotswold Way towards Bath, walking with a fence on your left and a hedge which soon becomes a wall on your right.

The wall on your right reverts to a hedge. Continue over a waymarked stile above and to the right of a small metal gate ahead. Reach a corner where a stile on your right gives unofficial access to the 714 ft summit of Kelston Round Hill. Turn left to follow the fenced Cotswold Way along Dean Hill with a view over Upper Weston on your left.

Join a rough lane very briefly to pass Pendean Farm on your right before bearing right with the signposted Cotswold Way across a stile. Walk with a hedge on your right, take a stile to a waymarked track and follow a fence on your right, above woodland on your left. Emerge along a ridge path overlooking Bath. This is Penn Hill (398 ft). Descend with a

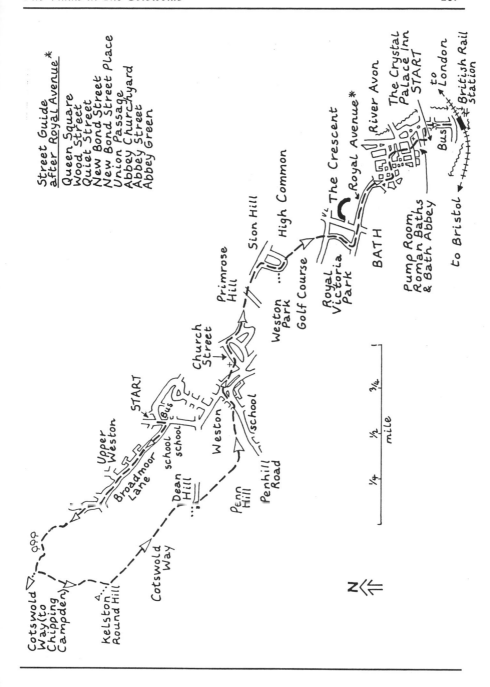

Street Guide
after Royal Avenue *

Queen Square
Wood Street
Quiet Street
New Bond Street
New Bond Street Place
Union Passage
Abbey Churchyard
Abbey Street
Abbey Green

Cotswold Way (to Chipping Campden)

Kelston Round Hill

Cotswold Way

Upper Weston

START

Broadmoor Lane

school

school

Dean Hill

Penn Hill

Weston

school

Penhill Road

Church Street

Primrose Hill

Sion Hill

Weston Park

Golf Course

High Common

The Crescent

Royal Avenue *

Royal Victoria Park

River Avon

BATH

Pump Room,
Roman Baths
& Bath Abbey

The Crystal Palace Inn
START

Bus

to London

British Rail Station

to Bristol

N

¼   ½   ¾
mile

hedge on your left to bear left over a waymarked stile in it. Descend to a stile in the fence at the foot of the field. Go ahead over playing fields to the far right corner ahead. Here, a kissing gate beside a signpost gives access to steps which lead down to Penhill Road.

Turn left along the pavement and go left with Penhill Road at a fork opposite Greenbank Gardens. Use a zebra crossing to go ahead over a road and bear right with the signposted Cotswold Way. Take the traffic-free Church Street to All Saints Church.

Pass All Saints Church on your left and leave its churchyard by a gap in the far wall. Turn left with the signposted Cotswold Way up Church Road. This becomes a path and you turn right at its top. Take the signposted Cotswold Way along the pavement of Purlewent Drive. Bear left at a triangle of grass, again with the Cotswold Way signpost to reassure you, to go up a cul-de-sac and take an enclosed footpath on your left. This path beads right to reach a squeeze stile. Continue with a hedge and a wall on your right down to a waymarked stile in the corner ahead. Cross the stile and follow a fence on your right to a kissing gate. Go up an enclosed path to the road at Primrose Hill.

Cross the road to continue up the path ahead, which has a metal handrail attached lo the wall on your right. Go ahead when you reach Summerhill Road, then turn right with the signposted Cotswold Way down Sion Hill. Follow this road as it bends left at the bottom. Reach the corner where it turns left uphill again and leave it by bearing right down a fenced path across High Common. Beware of low-flying golf balls!

Continue across a road to enter Royal Victoria Park. Follow the pavement of the road ahead and bear left to the Victoria Monument. Cross a road to go ahead up Royal Avenue. Notice Royal Crescent on your left. Emerge from the park to go right to Queen Square. Pass this on your left and turn left to reach Wood Street. Continue up Quiet Street, bear right up New Bond Street and turn right down New Bond Street Place. Maintain this direction down Union Passage, cross Cheap Street and reach the Abbey Churchyard. You may like to visit the abbey, on your left.

Continue by crossing York Street to go down Abbey Street to Abbey Green. The Crystal Palace Inn is on your right.